THE SHOVEL

THE SHOVEL

COLIN BROWNE

TALONBOOKS

Talonbooks
P.O. Box 2076, Vancouver, British Columbia, Canada V6B 3S3
www.talonbooks.com

Typeset in Adobe Garamond and printed and bound in Canada.
Printed on 100% post-consumer recycled paper.

First Printing: 2007

The publisher gratefully acknowledges the financial support of the Canada Council for the Arts;
the Government of Canada through the Book Publishing Industry Development Program; and the
Province of British Columbia through the British Columbia Arts Council and the Book Publishing
Tax Credit for our publishing activities.

Library and Archives Canada Cataloguing in Publication

Browne, Colin, 1946–
    The shovel / Colin Browne.

Poems.
ISBN 978-0-88922-574-9

    I. Title.

PS8553.R69S46 2007   C811'.54   C2007-901067-9

For my mother, Kythé

'We're too tired to remember.'
23 September 2006

Many thanks to the editors of the following publications: *71(+) for GB* (Jean Baird, David McFadden, George Stanley), above/ground press (rob mclennan), *The Capilano Review* (Jenny Penberthy) and *Open Letter* (Frank Davey, Nicole Markotic, Susan Rudy); to Marian Penner Bancroft, Pascal Breton, Hugh Brody, Kythé Browne, Sue Browne, Keith Donovan, Robin Garland, Linton Garner, Gerald Peary, Peter Quartermain, Colin and Graham Ritchie, Lisa Robertson, Fred Wah, Anna Wang; to Tom Cone, Karen Matthews and David Pay for *Song Room*; and to composer Neil Weisensel, soprano Susanna Browne, tenor Frederik Robert and baritone Michael Walker.

... what troops
Of generous boys in happiness thus bred ...
Went from the North and came from the South,
With golden mottoes in the mouth ...

Herman Melville, 'On the Slain Collegians' (1866)

Oum Kalthoum: A Beneficial Trauma

To all those castrated by under-development and occupation, she was saying that she loved them. She sings as for you alone, and in this love as deep as valleys and the ocean floor, the fellah and the prime minister found, each, what forgives all sins and recycles the son in the grace of the mother.

Erotic being, like the soufis, she reconciled the flesh and the spirit. She has been this century's thread. I heard her when I was twelve in the Grand Theatre of Beirut. It was a beneficial trauma.

Then, I followed her: in Cairo, where on the first Thursday of each month she made people leave home with a transistor radio, or they gathered at night in shops to listen to her in their long and white robes. Listening to her songs, which lasted for four or five hours, I heard the Nile moan and the human species give birth. In the divisions which break a world and make it explode, she was the unity we had.

Etel Adnan, 'In the Heart of the Heart of Another Country'

history

something nosing about in the dry arbutus leaves at dawn
something trying to get through the fence

A Man Addresses the Madonna

Shut up your scarf! You aren't a horse.
Do you know why I am laughing?

it was in an elm for mine
for mine, a ditch

in a camas blue dawn
my husband touched me

for the first time in months
my daughter, in the phlox

gathering seeds for
a school assignment

mine, picking violets
across the river

mine, on the tide
my son was never found

ammo

~~infinite~~
~~immense~~
~~empyreal~~
~~ethereal~~
~~arterial~~
~~bacterial~~
~~imperial~~
~~venereal~~
~~aerial~~
~~narial~~
~~sidereal~~
~~celestial~~
~~bestial~~
~~boreal~~
~~sensorial~~
~~fossorial~~
~~tonsorial~~
~~purgatorial~~
~~historical~~
~~ineluctable~~
~~innumerable~~
~~incalculable~~
~~irreducible~~
~~insensible~~
~~apprehensible~~
~~celestial~~
~~bestial~~
~~vestal~~
~~vestigial~~
~~cerulean~~
~~stellar~~
~~boolean~~
~~bending~~

~~numinous~~
~~luminous~~
~~voluminous~~
~~leguminous~~
~~blue~~
~~inky~~
~~starry~~
~~sapphire~~
~~sundering~~
~~thundering~~
~~elastic~~
~~plastic~~
~~sargassic~~
~~spinozic~~
~~metazoic~~
~~epiblastic~~
~~anapaestic~~
~~hyacinthian~~
~~nuagey~~
~~zenithy~~
~~vaulty~~
~~verismic~~
~~vertiginous~~
~~hieratic~~
~~heraldic~~
vasty

Apes You Sought

What do you do with your beautiful, young, freckled mind?
                                                    Duke Ellington

Apes you sought. To eat? To woo? Won't seize? There are herring tons to displace, tree rings,
      the furious tempi of the brine.
Was it kin you sought? Is your plastic sack assez? What each soul amounts to: a quart and a half of
      splintered mash. A milk truck
can deliver a consequential town before noon. Tommy Franks, I know you're putting in the days.
      Who's for the Hugo von
Hofmannsthal hotel? We're not mealy or fussy, but I've booked a flight on the Belgian linens.
      Who'd demur, even with
pinkeye? 'I'm getting the hell out of here,' says a cloud to my Mum as she reaches for a sleeve of
      Sleeman's. But Sarnia
was ours; we fertilized everyone in that county except the dogs, which our gang refused to ranch,
      to their credit, some say.
How that crowd sniggered behind its knuckles. But when we pulled the plug the loam was
      smoking. Abaft with your reptile
straight-waistcoats; the ape's skinned. It's William Thomas Strayhorn I spy in Charlie Ray's stuffy
      East Liberty joint, in 1937,
'an upholstered sewer,' Frank Bolden liked to call it. Saturday nights, on the break, Billy would
      scramble upstairs to catch
Camel Caravan, with Teddy Wilson, the notes knotting and exploding like starlings in a sockeye sky,
      and Strayhorn,
tracking that left hand, charting the changes in eternity somewhere between *thinking* and *listening*
      to thinking. Sweet Pea
drank it all in, down to the swung semi-colon. Back on the bandstand he'd stir up his own
      mirages, calling out chords as
the hoods made woo. On good nights The Tophatters healed the broken world lost in the dunes.
      Curly, two weeks ago,
on the familiar blade of Octopus Point, hunting mowitch when an old black bear surprised him in
      the trees along the logging road
as the first Cruise missiles excavated the heart of Baghdad. He flapped his arms, yelled a warning
      and pushed on, pondering

the Spotted Chevrotain. Apollinaire, with the motto 'I fill with wonder,' exclaimed—drowning
in the Spanish flu—'Save me, Doctor!
I want to live. I've still so much to say.' A little later, Curly hears branches snap, leaves crackle
overhead. The bear
pushes off into the air. Watching it, Curly thinks, I've got one shot. November 18th, 1963.
Marilyn Monroe is dead.
A Ba'athist coup in Iraq has liquidated several thousand sons and fathers called Communists. The
C.I.A. is pressing forward
with its anti-Nobel campaign against Pablo Neruda. Cyrillic translations of the 'Four Quartets'
have been parachuted into
the U.S.S.R. in an attempt to promote chronic depression among the population, perhaps to
stimulate a little consumer
therapy. That afternoon, Duke Ellington and Paul Gonsalves pose unconvincingly with a *narghile*
on their State Department tour
of Iraq, near Ctesiphon, where in 1915 Dick Ritchie's beautiful red-lipped body was shovelled
into the Tigris. Click. Ellington
sits in for a ruminant on the corn grinder. Click. It was a model coup; Mobil and Bechtel have
their contracts, the Kurds are
on the run. The boys in the band have been briefed. They've been told to act like free men, to
speak their minds. It's enough
to make a cat clam up. The next night, in Baghdad, just before curtain time, Strayhorn and
Arthur Logan get word something's
cooking. They scramble up onto the roof of Khuld Hall. Disgruntled Ba'athist hard-liners in
surplus MiGs are buzzing the city,
winkling out former colleagues beneath the stars. Click. Click. Sweet Pea's Brownie tracks the old
jets roaring through the
Mesopotamian night toward the President's palace. Explosions bloom on the avenues. Next day
in Beirut, Ellington's
interviewed by the press. '*Ça swinguait, mon cher. Ça swinguait,*' he declares. 'Those cats were
swinging, man.' One doesn't

21

routinely concur with Valéry and his pet ichthyophageses, though a lark t'would be to perch
there, smitten by the self-assigned
privilege of parting the grubby veil, but can you remain smugly detached when he declares,
après Leonardo,
'Artistic observation can attain an almost mystical depth. The objects on which it falls lose their
names. Light and shade form
very particular systems …?' But then he's off again with the blancmange of the soul's spreadsheet
and the travails of the scab-infested
inner self. I thought we'd ditched whingers for brushed-steel cyberspace. Question is, does my
little dog know its stick's name?
Who wouldn't want to strap on a jet-pack and roll the barbeque back to the pre-linguistic
riverbank? Would you recognize
your footprint in the clay? The purging of the Iraqi 'reds' was a C.I.A. job, the agency having
arranged for a transmitter
in Kuwait to broadcast their names. Who would you, with impunity, do in? What would it take?
Just a purifying little flense?
Strayhorn lived for four more years. He was composing until the end, waltzing that lousy cancer
around the hospital room,
rubbing its swollen face in love. Curly kept his cool. The bear landed in front of him, snarling. A
Beaver cleared the firs, the bear charged,
Curly shot his bullet into its heart. Calling to mind its tide pool eyes, the midden shell teeth, Curly
said if he'd of been that bear's
supper, he'd of been the gristle that did the old boy in. Consequences lie dormant until stirred up.
Think sea-monkeys. A year
before the tour, Sweet Pea recalled hearing Ellington for the first time in Pittsburgh, in June 1934.
The band 'played "The Rape
of a Rhapsody", that was the name of the number. Oh, it was wonderful … that's what really got
me. He had a chord which I
have never discovered, I haven't heard it since, I couldn't figure this chord out. I went home
after going to see this show

at the Penn Theatre …, and I couldn't figure out what was in that chord … it was just wonderful.'
      In October 1914, near

St. Juliaan, bordering a sector soon to be designated 'Vancouver' by Canadians dug in there—in
      six months the German 4th Army

will release 135 tonnes of chlorine gas in ten minutes on an evening breeze—waves of flaxen-
      haired young men in clean shorts,

the *Wandervogel,* link arms and march through ripe corn toward the Vickers machine guns
      singing of chastity's rewards.

Breton's dream, ten years later, in which Apollinaire's shadow admits to no interest in a stranger
      named Apollinaire.

A map, you say, to find your way out of here? Sorry, light and shade present very particular
      systems. In the dappled garden,

ancient roses raise their fists in mutiny. A bee awakes, lays a buzz in your ear. And this audacious
      decoy—the mutable, teeming

world of chords and branes you've named to make—turns on bristles, a song, a salpinx. Want in?
      Follow the mouse turds

Home

for my mother

Asking, 'How? How will I know?'

Asking, 'Do you know if that crow flying out of the blizzard has a reason?'

Asking, 'What is unhappiness?'

Asking, 'Why is a man cursed for being eaten by a lion?' Is it because the lion becomes what a man is: divided?

The fire bringer said, 'Wretched is the body that is dependent on a body, and wretched is the soul that is dependent on these two.'

How small fractures insist, hungers, habits, vigilance.

I cannot tell if this is a guy world or a bird world.

Asking, 'Why is he anathema, this eaten man?'

Like a siskin to the feeder, swinging with the sway of redwings fleeing.

What if you encountered no one to whom you could speak of God? If no one showed up to assure you that it was not only you?

Asking, 'Are you zealous? Would you give your life to keep one from becoming two?'

The sword wielder said, 'On the day when you were one you became two.'

On this green shelf, I, whom she made to seek the beating heart of the world, the beating heart of undivided love.

My mother, of hers: 'She was an unhappy, unhappy woman for many years after that.'

This makes her happy in bursts between 1886 and 1916 and not again for fifty-six years. Goethe
       calculated that a lifetime might fairly expect to enjoy two weeks of happiness. Which bird
       would you be?

It was not entirely Scotland's fault.

Asking, 'If you knew you were one, and pretended to be two, thinking that's how it's done,
       would you be two, or one?'

You would be three. But that cloud won't shut up. That cloud looks like a spaniel.

To see is to be and cease to be one.

Ta guele.

Two regions of the brain hatch neurons: the olfactory bulb and the hippocampus, its ridges
       echoing with the discharges of perpetual electrical storms, its dark skies lighting up with
       each new countenance, every contorted promontory. When my mother spots a knowable
       breed in the sky she generates a transient memory in this renewable limbic tissue, an
       eager net cast into the blue. Astride a seahorse she beholds the shore.

Seeing is also remembering. When she sees eyes on an oval drawn on a placemat, she pencils in
       tears like diamonds.

It is not the same as you remembering. You remember you are remembering.

The warrior said, 'When you make the two one, and when you make the inside like the outside and the outside like the inside, and the above like the below, and when you make the male and the female one and the same, so that the male not be male nor the female female; and when you fashion eyes in place of an eye, and a hand in place of a hand, and a foot in place of a foot, and a likeness in place of a likeness; then will you enter.'

She fought hard to wrench herself out of time; she is nearly there. She navigates by trees. Last year she pointed out a cherry from 1929. She speaks to seagulls. She'll never shop again. Sometimes it seems everything will be torn apart like clouds. She is present and ready and alone. She believes she is the only one.

She has never breathed a word of this.

The destroyer said, 'Show me the stone which the builders have rejected. That one is the cornerstone.'

Sophia.

She would say she is nearly home now. She would say, 'That is how.'

Anagram Loop, May 2006

the pen
in her bruised
orange, pink and blue
wanted
what?
was
was it?
what was?
but like

then, the

blotch
a little patch of
ants' legs

an ox-
like a

she sits up

from kaos
an alphabet

my mother
will not
be broken

Carlyle Square

for Fred Wah

It
found
me

at the green
jamb
of an open

pane
one
bleak

St. Lucy's
morning,
a scent of

arbutus
bark
salt

hot
thimbleberries
and

that stubborn
subaltern
poverty—

its rationed
Yes
and

No
my mother's
yes

and
no—
the music

at the heart
of my
earliest

thinking.
Diphthongs, grave
and

wilful, greened
in Carlyle
Square

where Sitwell
sat.
Two wheels

that June
spoke gravel,
a wee burn

its gleam
and
turbulence

prized by
stick racers,
gurgled

green fields
across
the road

from
Moniak
Castle,

honeysuckle
nursed us
on skin warm

stones
until my name
was called,

my mother's
voice
the furrow

my words
still dance
through,

and when
I say
I hear myself

thinking
it is my
mother's

voice
I hear,
clear,

lonely
music at
the heart of

a shy
and
fugitive

love
that cracked
a lion's heart.

Listen: that
love is you
speaking,

you thinking
even when
you forget

that love
this love
her love.

Decomposition

Oystercatcher, pearlescence! She! Overtaken by snouted creatures, with crow hush in yellow cedars and the *ghimel*-streaks yew bark smudges on their haunches in the fidgeting bluff-scraping dawn as, sniffing one another, they reckon up the parlous paracosm—what you longingly christen

The Visible World—which is, a mercy, incomplete, an open throat, a charred ditch spanned by unpeeled sticks; for some, she thinks, such as I, love's epic is limned in limbs, white and with a knee; for others, the Axle of Contempt, or the Name of the Beloved, spelled out in bitter wands of

tansy—thrillingly unknowable; take, for example, bone ash, alchemy's midwife (*phosphate* being after its fashion hermaphroditic—or a C, for *calcination*, or *caduceus, corbel* [a smile of sorts, or a little band], or *coquina, coral*—'a bright reddish mass of edible ovaries'—tucked into by the Giant

in the Human Heart—sans bib, cup or frown—in the heat of oxytocic mayhem—and how the involuntary ramming of yourself against another in the fervent hope you'll disappear scars with thrilling cries the smooth hull of The Invisible gliding into the churning lock), rousing the green

imperium of gorse, the holy Book of Limestone, the love-scented clevis or grater of flesh coming upon itself after trapeze-loads of abject accretion to find little more than a prized but useless dusting of corpse-crumbs in a rush to sprout stalks for strays to mark, or so she thinks she thinks

on the veranda above the devil's club and blackberry suckers, it's January 1939, the rain is steady, the sea is grey, her body is vanishing (not only as a colonial artifice), we're ten years west of Babs Gonzales, and the drumming intensifies each night, insistent, quickening, summoning she knows she'll never know what but she can imagine the carbon from which the night was cast, roaring sparks, the cedar, the triumphant peal of all she's not, and she thinks, 'I know nothing. I don't know their kids' names. Do they speak to their god, have they seen his bandages?' In London, she

thought she saw Dr. Freud in his garden through a hedge of laurel and cigar smoke. What she hopes she longs for seeks an analogue beyond longing in the whirling star skin, in the streaming water, in the green walls pressing here where she can no longer hold up her bones. She is fluid,

unable to contain her self, the turbulence of back eddies sweeps her down, she rushes through a turbine of song, her mouth, trembling, words welling out of her cracks, fish and animal shapes, the horned owl, the cries of fire in the sundering blackness. To be candled by a god, to be taken!

Loft No Stain

1.

I hope I'm in the right, vestibule.
Wanting to ask if anyone.
Springs. Like bindweed, from posse
to passé. I've been
I swear this wave of it.
Of ivy, but pinked,
pretty in its
pileated vestry. And fastic!
Invasive. Would
I knew wits vame.
But, seriously,
you're bucking, well, not bucking,
snipping up kindling and. Look, another
root oven in the air. V's at
firebox intervals. Who couldn't?
Cadden't. Waldn't
variegate?
Grows bog. Not in bricky Vancouver,
Meredith, I didn't. No, we possumed
to Malamud's stone in Mt. Auburn
Gerry lay down and
loved him in the splendid.
I hue, I'm a sojourner myself.
Yes, the famous shed and
moocher's carcass
of water. Here's
a rock from a root.
Toss it on.
We loft no stain. A tern,
yet. Many times over and
never and yes.
I'm a spelunker here myself.

My limb's
at the swimming hole,
-so

2.
Dowser? I wonder.
If it's forgetting you're
off the hake. I mean.
It'll blaw o'er.
The furrows in the brae
rinsed the slate.
Dr. Freud's screaming
chasm
the sparrow
that peeped twice
at 0315
in the vines
outside my window.
The son taken out
into the orchard
and shot
by his father
for love.
The heaps of clothing
picked through.
We'll repeat
ourselves
if we don't forget.
Is biological determinism?
I'm amnesia's child
with A.D.D.

a Y-shaped dick, and
terminal decay.
Why?
What?
Pink chrysanthemums
spill down
or I'm
haemorrhaging

Discharge: Kodaks from Galilee

1.

Lads I frolicked with
in the desert, my little skin.
An offer of Abel in an eddy.
Hinge between
him and my golden hairs.
Say your hosanna,
admitting you're neither free
nor clear.
The friend who saved the day
lost the night.

2.

A cable or two from an armoured lorry
the lake is wasting away.
Here, fish forge patriots,
each bite
a bouillabaisse
of saint's shite,
lover's spurt,
leper's pelt,
Templar bone;
the scalded, the shriven
are flecks of foam
in a velouté of
flayed skin
next stop,
next of kin.

Bon appetit.

3.

Early on, with my adversary asleep, one enters and takes my hand, arm and suppurating eye. It's
Judith M., she is venting. Why are these little splotches here? An onion's tossed down the lane, a
shedding urn. A strike subdues the splotches. These splotches are building settlements in those

splotches. One passes and says, '*C'est toi! Allium cepa*, launched and rolling, is a watch pinned to
a dandy's lining. What shed? A town's melon. I've got a list no one has seen before, Judith, not
even the hanged boy of Halifax has wept these tears. I'll lunge into the fray at the fork of lustral

bathing to barge that log house up the river. I could not find his name on Mount Scopus. When
Enid and Dick drew the curtains in Crowborough they rolled their lives back along the Goose
Lake Road. Mespot sun in Dick's brown eyes. The General whipped his dog Spot then ordered

a charge with bayonets fixed. After the butchery and top secret trenches of Desert Sabre, 'Elvis',
as HVT-1 was in his spider hole yclept, had the Basra Memorial dismantled, trucked to a plain
near Nasiriyah, and rebuilt, panel-by-panel. Father, why me? Mother, please, mak my bed soon.

Dick's on Panel Ten, one of 40,500 in the Commonwealth War Graves database: 'Son of Thomas
and Alice, husband of Enid Kathleen, of The Shack, Crowborough, Sussex.' He was twenty-four.
It was November 1915. Roland Barthes was ten days old. Judith, why am I telling you this? In the
British cemetery at Basra, the old occupiers are back and sprucing up, shooing away wild dogs.
The planet demands bones. Judith, is that all I have to say? I am becoming careless. This face I'm
saving is borrowed. This courage a collapsing shack, this bag of flesh a splotchy Gehenna.

4.

I've naught to add. No camel. No legs, no teeth. No stall. That old man, gone. My old man,
gone. I can't even tell you nothing. Read the *Star-Advertiser*. A dog blurs. Batoche is shelled.
Everyone had a dog or two, but why bring them along? The smoke from the nine-pounders
clings to the ground and is breathed in by buttercups.

He told me at the eightieth birthday party that the resisters were all obnoxious, bad apples, every one. Several hundred were shoved into a camp among the arbutus trees. Don't feel sorry for them, he said. Their leader, he said, was out for what he could get.

The Kingdom of God is here. You don't need a flyblown lunatic, he said. I put up my hand. Go to hell, I said.

Bitterroot the smoke dug.

5.
Quail beneath olive branches, sunny
between the crawler tracks.

6.
tolerable = meaningful

No Nag

That was no year, that was a nag
I rode full bore until I was sore
afraid of everything. That was no
everything, that was justice.

That was no justice, that was
just I see what you mean
now, but that was no now,
that was no, that was

no no, that was the tower
the dukes stood in, in linen,
in rose. That was no rose
that was just a tall pink lady

and a man who crept out
of the sea for ages, who got along
by squashing just about
everything. They became

champions of the world,
as bad as they were good,
and God-people, bad as God was
in their hands, but they had

hands and they used them,
and man could they sing,
and were they clever
in bed!

They flayed hoarse Rocinante
with the Rubicon-stained hooves
in the fo'c'sle, which is a soup,
a pope and a plank. And that's no

doomed piano score, buddy,
that's them pounding
the black keys and that
triumphant crack and roar

is the foul, tar-spitting
fire ship of the old year
sinking as the skookum ketch
of next casts off.

You're being pulled
into the flames?
Bend your green legs,

                    jump

The Pool

of what you call knowing mackerels over. The air cools. This prelude's a shot at set dec, but what have we got instead? Mere approximations in the reeds. Fetch the barney. Encourage your feral Forerunner to pose in tongues like clouds scraped by clamshells of iridescent solar nudging.

Scruffy roots stuffed into his pouch. What's with the five details? Animal hair where he's without, hide diaper, the locust legs, etc. He irritates the self-reflexive sons of light with their minimalism and paradoxical sublimities. He stinks in the heat. I love that in is out and out is in. One whines:

'We enter the Holy Book at aleph. We bathe where no water flows. We lug our shit to the jackal's wadi. If we are sons of women it was not our idea. We invite the triumph of the shovel in the dreadful day to come. And that hyena, that boy we left to shrivel, lopes out of the desert, smeared

with what was within, howling, and they fondle him, the loveless, the gullible, the sycophants of Sol Invictus; they submit!' The unfortunate scuffle is over who'll glory in the Final Mayhem. How does one survive a wordstorm of woe? The Forerunner undermines the swish with ribby scrawn

and the five repulsive details. Surrender to words, and they melt away (as even with a freshening breeze, in Melville, the Encantadas recede). We'd invite that know-it-all Enki in, but do we covet his tilapia suit? One day you'll open the hatch and I'd stock up on doves. Salt crust in the rushes,

March ice on Lac St. Louis. What is more Red than the he-goat's tool? What is more vulgar than mindless hallelujahs in the rushes to the brides of Yes and the bridegrooms of No, bless their commissar hides? Picture Chagall in Vitebsk in 1918, the commissar of Fine Arts. 'My eyes,' he

wrote, 'glowed with administrative fire.' No, and yes. In the anchorites' defence, they're appalled by a prophet without a book. The cousin who hied the lice eater to the *midbar* after appearing with his mother on a cloud was being strategic. Chagall was ambushed by the revolution's immolation

of the imagination. So what if those mountaintops are snipped out of cardboard rectangles in pocket packs of Kleenex mounted with furious backlight on a *trompe l'oeil* card table? There's a kind of hush all over the world. da Vinci's brush uncovered in the matted bonesack a luminous polymorph, neither brazen nor prudent—innocent as a fish—as a lover fearless, lavish in his sensibilities, a faun, an hermaphroditic rupture in a beast's cape, a dreamily priapic Bacchus. The binary's fraud is here laid bare. For Caravaggio, envoy to the court of Orphée's Temple, eye-

confectioner, the Baptizer comes in every posture: *here* the rough and tumble laddie with take-me-now eyes and the ram's thick horn; *there*, the sitter with a drooping sheep's foot no one could mistake for a sheep's foot. One, bird-boned and less coarse, pouts. Another, lusty and muscled,

surely cost him—at least in heartbreak bucks. Pleasure may have consoled them, all three, and wine, and what kindness or ransom obtained. At Sepphoris in the Galilee a mosaic Dionysus bends an elbow with a Heracles just up the *viae rusticae* from the pool where the orphaned hermit

shook his staff, as dismayed as I by this horizon of flesh. I'll take a rain check on decay. Language tracks advance and withdrawal; the present is inconceivable: a wave on an inky pool. We're the lung. *Bangiophyceae* and *florideophyceae* churn the lustre. Beyond: icy darkness with Latinate suffixes.

Barthes, speaking of an 'uttering (not an utterance) through which the subject plays out its division through dispersal, casts themself obliquely across the scene of the blank page,' sought protraction, the fold in the bend in the tempest of flesh we crave, my sweet. Should that be temple? Barthes'

'*obliquely*' offers a theological solution: subject abdicates subjectivity. Solution in dissolution. The pool as a blank blue page. Demons sup at his lesions, slaves to his delirium. Pilgrims buzz about the scarlet, aortic fountains, the cylindrical stump. At least a dozen wizened, mouldering heads lie

squirreled away from Damascus to Poitou, an incontestable carte blanche for exterminatory congregations; his nibs' old knob gave 'em the nod. The blessed virgin Thekla carried a forefinger into the Alps; a withered hand tours Russia with V. Putin in a jewel-encrusted chest. How many

have been disembowelled in his name? Young Salome and Herodias, the garrison wife, took the fall. The Podromos had served his purpose; he'd become an impediment. According to the Mishna, a locust is comestible when its wings eclipse its body. Who knows whose end one serves?

The law is a weathervane (and knows its master). As Salome dances stars fill the pool. Trees crack open. Drums, cymbals, psalteries ring; desire is a magnificent engine. The executioner insists he's following orders. He begs forgiveness from the bleeding wreck, the rival, who, by 1430, promises

'with a cheerful face' to intercede on the poor man's behalf. Idolaters and lunatics weep to hear the cleaving. The neck that wears the head is not the head that wears the crown. According to Josephus, his 'disembodied spirit' keeps watch to this day to expose evil in all its guises. After

vanquishing all this we thought we'd won. We did, but we were not who we thought we were.

what I took for war
opened the door

what I clutched in love
a glove

what I said at the end
I'll bend

I could only applaud
the vanishing god

What's To Know

0. It's invisible.

1. Why are you squatting here with your Sharpie?

2. A strategy: ignite the arc between things.

3. The arc is everything in motion just before it is.

4. Back to Bishop Berkeley.

5. Mitts off the volume.

6. In the estuary, declaiming in the Diespecker style, up to his sock tops, the dark-haired Earle B. longs for a share of greatness.

7. One ought to ask, pointedly, 'How are the valves?' Everything else is gravy.

8. Recall Wallace Stevens cautioning Richard Wilbur that publication in *The New Yorker* would be the kiss of death. These thousands of empty shells.

9. He loves to hear night splashing in the lake.

10. Our own Golden Jubilee poet, A.M. Stephens, was devoted to hygiene and family planning. Make that an obedient, economically productive family with *all* its marbles and valves intact.

11. Settlement. When water sinks.

12. Transmission. When water rises.

13. Homonymy is insufficient. What seems to have stuck in their craw was his lunch: roots, corms, fruit, bugs. He hung out in those hyena-skin britches? 'Salt Peanuts' is a kind of love.

14. 'Please make entry soon or be disconnected.'

15. I know you won't be smug about Stephens and his eugenophilia. You above all know who covets the spotless jodhpurs.

16. 'I envy (in a manner of speaking) any man who has the time to prepare something like a book and who, having reached the end, finds the means to be interested in its fate or in the fate which, after all, it creates for him.' André Breton, *Nadja.*

17. In those early years I made few bucks on prosthetics before going into refrigeration.

18. Grab the crab captains' sperm count will you, Dan?

19. In that little corner store in the middle of the block near the original KSW, with his back to me, our champion. How swiftly he slid his magazine behind another when I spoke his name.

20. When I opened my eyes all the capitals were red.

21. Henry Ford added up 670 operations on the line that could be performed by legless men and 715 suitable for those with a single arm. You one-legged? Screw on that peg and get down here. He's got 2,637 jobs you'd ace. That's a third of a Model T.

22. I am the face on your head.

23. These woods have their ghosts. This town also, though most are dry cleaning bags.

24. The egg: the hand, the killing cold. The knife: the crack. The pan: the chute. The yolk: the moon. The white: snow banks on the Lièvre. The crispy fringes: loons.

25. Come to think of it, the bearded poet picking a Tim Bit out of a pail at Jericho looked familiar.

26. Dissing the Abyss. There are lucrative contracts to be had, my son.

27. Down there by the withered sedge, that was a sick business, man, that rhizomic coupling or whatever it was, but, you know, stripped down, and like I always say it wasn't until the E.J. Pratt congress that it really took off for us.

28. Ross: 'What key?' Linton: 'Oh, 'round B flat.'

29. 'I inherited my poetry.' Bialik

30. I noticed that the Earle Birney at the Chocoholic's Midnight Madness on even nights plays Pound at the Wyndham Lewis tea on non-Shrove Tuesdays.

31. The Baptizer's halo is the lover's rut.

32. Céline in Detroit, 1926: 'We saw the hiring process: the candidates the management likes best are those who are the most down-and-out, physically and psychologically ... The doctor ... confided to us that what they really wanted was chimpanzees.'

33. I embrace the useless, for it's the present I'll never know, the wind that never ceases you call God.

34. I'd rather bad authority than good authority.

35. Carmen McRae to Linton Garner, the first time he sat in with her on piano. After two bars she stopped, turned around and glared. 'Linton,' she said, 'I *know* the tune!'

Who Lester Called Clem

for Linton Garner (1915–2003)

One day last year he asked if I knew why African-Americans were not worked up about the threat of terrorism. 'A little thing called the Ku Klux Klan,' he said.

He kept a little black book bound by elastic bands that listed every gig he'd ever played. In January 1947 he was with Mr. B. in New York.

When he got on with the Eckstine band he replaced the piano player. 'I can remember his nickname,' he said. '*Stick Carrier*.' He grinned. 'That's special language,' he said, 'you wouldn't understand.' Stick Carrier was the guy who'd announce when the bus pulled into Philadelphia that he'd left his tuxedo in New York. He never had enough cash for his dinner bill. He somehow was always next door for the first few numbers of every show, and was not missed.

When he was a teenager Linton played piano at Crawford Grill Number One on Wylie Avenue at Fullerton in Pittsburgh. 'I knew a few chords by then,' he said. He loved to flow in behind the singer on a bed of luxurious notes that were to a melody what a honeybee is to a candle. If you're wondering where Bop began, look here.

Count Basie arrived in Pittsburgh for a couple of weeks in 1935 with the first black band to play in a downtown hotel. After the broadcast the boys came up to the Crawford Grill and jammed until two. Then it was across the street for breakfast at the Wolverine. They were kids, creating something. A nation with a body to replace America.

During that time no one slept. Linton knew where a stand-up piano was so one night he and the saxophone player went over and played duets until ten in the morning. When he got home his mother asked, 'Where you been?' 'Playing piano with Lester Young,' he said. 'Hmmm,' she said, 'who's that?' Linton was still a teenager. 'Count Basie I've heard of,' she said, 'but who's Lester Young?'

Every night for two weeks. Clem. 'That was the name he gave me,' said Linton. 'I never knew why.'

Who does not fret about memory? I see it as a twentieth-century anxiety, but maybe everyone has always wanted to walk out into the desert and sleep under the cleansing stars. Memory is not a lump of something. It's a contractor hired for you when you were helpless, it never stops and it insists on building incomparable structures of sand—like a hive or a termite's nest—and now you stare at the roof and you know it will need to be replaced soon and you're the termite.

Of course this is the fallible, rebellious, knowable, self-deceiving, extroverted memory, not the deep, infallible memory over which you have no control—the kind stored in his fingers, for lack of a more technical way to articulate its methods. The infallible memory operates you as a medium, a transducer, an *instrument*, refining you as it goes about its mysterious, necessary work. The body's destiny is to become a circuit dedicated exclusively to this memory. When you say 'mind' it is your beautiful body you honour.

Days before he passed, sitting at the new piano in The Cellar, his fingers nudged an impromptu Paul Plimley tune into a haunting take on 'Summertime'. That was the metaphysics of the man. He could not help himself; well, he could, but why would he? Why close an opening door?

He was proud to say he always had a job, sometimes two. His first was on the Chicken Truck. It would pick up a load of hens and roosters at dawn and drive up and down the streets of East Liberty selling from house to house. Linton must have been about seven. When someone's mother picked out one of the birds, the driver pulled out his hatchet. The boy's job was to chase after that part of the hen that still had feet, that still knew the way home.

Face it, on this world my hold's
that of a wing
on the air.

We talk about Jesus every morning
after I insert my suppository.
My daughter drives
impatiently. I love her.

I love the tea in China.

The Order

His Dad was surveying roadbed
in the summer of 1914
up on the 123rd
at Cluculz Lake.
No one for the world gave a damn.
But they came straight down.
Scottie caught the next train to Montreal.
The old man signed up with
the 29th Battalion.
Tobin's Tigers.
Did I remember them?
Tallest guy in the Canadian Army?
Remember him?
Wasn't him.

One morning in France,
dodging a gale of shrapnel,
the platoon vaulted
into a nest of terrified German
boys who, being
more numerous
in their crater,
begged the Tigers to surrender.

Who were grateful
for the reprieve.
In their prison camp near Frankfurt
Hun guards, some badly stove in,
slipped in for coffee
after supper, sometimes.

There were among the Tigers Freemasons.
Every so often Fritz
hammered on the door
and called one by name.
By the next evening, his Dad
said, the man would be
in Switzerland.

I was fiddling in a clogged stream
at Jericho
in my fifty-ninth year.

On being invited to join the Vancouver Lodge in 1950
the son was taken aside
and told he was embarking
on the experience
of a lifetime.
'I didn't say I'd been
a gunner in the North Atlantic,'
he said, 'or on a freighter
off Zanzibar. I was ashore
in England for three
months loading ammunition.
One morning, in sailed a British cruiser.
A beauty.
I thought, "That's for me."
I wonder to this day,
why didn't I follow my heart?'

This Life

This life is a treasure.
You can't pretend
it's not. You can only
fall to your knees,
intoxicated.

Rejoice.

The woman on the inside page
dowsing herself with gasoline
is your sister. Cherish her.
This crouching man
is your brother.
Worship him.

His job is to destroy himself
and his family for you
as quickly, efficiently and profitably
as possible. His grandchildren
will be no liability thanks to recent
drug patent legislation.

Do you cherish this remarkable bargain?
Your otherworldly family needs to know soon
how you like your precious life.

March

my hose has
spring a leak

Noughts and Crosses

a crow

an Indian rubber ball

a bouncing clam

Fan your ember, Amber, I'm your anagram
of stench and guile, the vermilion bucks surge
to when markets sausage. Calling heat
down on the MERs this season is,
I kid you not, we'll murder the suckers. Here,
have a truffle. I am really me, a sea
bass swimming in corn oil and
soy Canadiense, amiga, scaly
and free from hormonal gleam.
When I smell genetic opportunity
I bilge. My hair shines.
Scarf another Wild Cherry, compadre.

Purvey'd in Charles II's
reign by 'a matron
of the name of Philips
at the Green Canister
in Half Moon Street...,'

what Scots pounded offal into
girls in the faubourgs cut
to size
'after, of course, much
manipulation
to make it thin
and supple'

capote anglaise

and the India rubber from Lilas?
Adventurers of all faiths
pronounced them ideal
for colonial penetration.

Kesey in the redwoods
packing his shotgun with
morning glory seeds
discharging them into the hills.

In the parade I play Gabriel Dumont.
At night I've that naughty red
thing in my pocket.

Palisades in
trees.

Palisades
of trees.

Céline: 'I have no interest
in trees.'

If I were to shout who would hear me ... out of the armies of angels?

Theo Angelopoulos, *Landscape in the Mist*

In anticipation of a son
he strangled his beloved,
effacing her name
from the stars.

Shekhinah, nautilus of love,
pray for us.

Eternity sucked.
He chafed at the covenant.
Let this be a lesson,
he told his decoy.

Nautilus of love,
pray for us.

I'm a trireme wanton. Bring me one of those
honey-coloured boys from Ithaca,
would-ja? Just joking. I'm a transcendental
nineteenth-century Canadian poet,
with a title split from logs. Hey, imagine Archibald
modelled from olives! Make that
flesh-tones, Sally, down by
the al-Lampman gardens.
The students in the Guangdong Academy of the Arts
shouting *Vagina!* one hundred times.
You had to be there.
Are the bushes only for customers?

I'm a trireme wanton. Bring me one of those
honey-coloured boys from Ithaca,
would-ja? Just joking. I'm a transcendental
nineteenth-century Canadian poet,
with a title split from logs. Hey, imagine Archibald
modelled from olives! Make that
flesh-tones, Sally, down by
the al-Lampman gardens.
The students in the Guangdong Academy of the Arts
shouting *Vagina!* one hundred times.
You had to be there.
Are the bushes only for customers?

Gristle, my darling.
The *Empress of India* rubs off.
Never oblige hookworm.
I think my heart is beating

Call me the Butcher of the Narrows.
I've the aristocratic neck,
a skookum little runabout,
my hair's not coarse,
I bring you God's love
and show the little shits
what's what,
bucking, limbing,
stringing wire,
in the dairy,
in the galley,
darning, picking,
romancing
the spade.

They pray too much,
the women.
Here's the trench for waste.
God does not want me to waste anyone.
You can't buy that view
for a million bucks.

Lamb, of Coleridge, '… he had a hunger for eternity.'

Before the insurrection they welcomed us
with convincing smiles but recently
our trucks have been stoned,
our people ridiculed.

We'll befriend them
to draw them out.
We're taking up positions
in the hills.
I once fell asleep in this green copse
under a harvest moon.
I alone among the leaders call it that.

1. *Did my brother Salim employ this new knife today? – Not, he did not employ it today, but yesterday.* 2. *The wells which our predecessors had digged were deeper than the wells which we have digged.* 3. *When our grand-father heard that my brother Salim hit our ass yesterday, he disapproved it.* 4. *My father vowed yesterday in the new mosque that he will dig a well near the mosque.* 5. *My sister saw last night in the dream that a venerable person has digged a well in this village near the mosque.* 6. *The noble Arabs used to send their children into the desert to strengthen their bodies and nerves there.* 7. *When my sister saw to-day that our mother has not yet return from Jerusalem, she became hopeless.* 8. *Shakir, do not employ this new ruler to-day, but employ that long ruler.* 9. *How many days stayed thy mother in this village last year? – She stayed here last year ten days.* 10. *How many wells did thy father dig in this village? – He digged here two wells.*

Jochanan Kapliwatzky, *Arabic Language and Grammar*, Part II.

I peeled off my skin,
found a flag and a king,
one, Jack, the other, George.
I was their arms
and eyes, the bruises
on their legs,
their little cocks
their sneers.
Many is the time they tried to off me.
What shall I do with my good intentions?

I stoned swans on the Serpentine,
shanghaied spiders
for little schooners
more stable than any father.
I shot seals for five bucks
a nose. I pit-lamped.
I guddled in the delta and watched
the demolition of everything I loved
by those who loved me.
What shall I do with my good intentions?

My father returned; not Malcolm's,
Mary's or Sam's.
His own screaming
woke him
in the New World.
And in the morning, with juncos
in the holly and holly berries
gleaming in the sun
it was as if nothing had happened at all.
What shall I do with my good intentions?

I opened my arteries to the wind.
We were a single aching animal.
I worked in the watershed
setting chokers.
When we made love I called it
the furnace. She shook my bones loose.
A mother, taking me inside her.
I pray she'll never leave me.
What shall I do with my good intentions?

In the new militias
we'll urge our pilots to be swift
and merciful.

In the coves of Half Moon Arm
our patrimony will not
be neutered by
loyalty
or sentiment.

An unhealthy set?
An untimely drop?
God turns his back.

Before I introduce them
to the Internal Hygiene Unit
I record the orphans' names.

during the hard days
a soft man settled on the river
and built a kippery
in a shack beside his own

they found him off
Sturgeon Bank
filleted

and the boy?

'Some people
develop
a taste
for things,'
he said,
squeezing my bad arm.
'That's how
it begins.'

Eden's plan: an armoured van.

Our advantage:
hemispheric division.
I encourage it in every boy.

Without it Half Moon Arm would be
a stinking tidal flat
clogged with scum,
our nation would succumb
to the venereal morbidity
of our inferiors,
our vitality would be
compromised.

Seize at will. Relinquish nothing.
It's for their own good.
Burn all orders,
use your advantage
to prosper.

The sea does not remember
the swimmer.

Concede the nettlesome truce.
Pay the fathers what they ask.
Steer clear of the mothers.

In two generations
everything
will be forgotten.

up the Narrows

down the Narrows

home
&
away

pray
&
prey

in God's country

I'm the coward you require,
the one deficient in civic courage.
I do the spin, the deference.
I was groomed thus,
a tool,
ashamed, and in
my own mind,
divine.

Hundreds of thousands of us:
obedient
creative
replaceable

deadly
in unison.

And the boy
with the torn neck?

That was me.

Diplomacy, Vancouver Island, 1845–1865

H.M.S. Alert, 17 gun first class screw corvette, eight 32-pound smooth bore guns on each broadside, one fitted up as a bow-chaser

H.M.S. Amphitrite, 24 gun sixth rate spar-decked frigate, sail

H.M.S. Bacchante, 50 gun flagship, Pacific Station

Beaver, H.B.C. paddle steamer, Brigantine-rigged, 4 brass cannons

H.M.S. Brisk, 14 gun screw sloop

H.M.S. Cameleon, 17 gun screw sloop, twelve 32-pound six-inch cannon, four 40-pound eight-inch Armstrong rifled cannon, one 40-pound ten-inch Armstrong rifled cannon on a rotating carriage

H.M.S. Charybdis, 21 gun screw corvette

H.M.S. Clio, 22 gun screw corvette

H.M.S. Constance, 50 gun fourth rate frigate, sail

H.M.S. Cormorant, 6 gun paddle wheel first class steam sloop

H.M.S. Daedalus, 42 gun fifth rate frigate, sail

H.M.S. Daphne, 18 gun sixth-rate frigate, sail

H.M.S. Devastation, 6 gun paddle wheel first class steam sloop

H.M.S. Dido, 18 gun corvette, sail

H.M.S. Driver, 6 gun paddle wheel first class steam sloop

Enterprise, H.B.C. paddle steamer

H.M.S. Explorer, schooner

H.M.S, Fisgard, 42 gun fifth rate frigate, sail

H.M.S. Forward, 3 gun steam-powered gunboat, one 32-pound rifled cannon aft on pivoting carriage loaded with exploding shrapnel, two 24-pound howitzers amidships

H.M.S. Ganges, 84 gun second-rate ship of the line, flagship, Pacific Station, sail

H.M.S. Grappler, 3 gun steam-powered gunboat, one 32-pound rifled cannon aft on pivoting carriage loaded with exploding shrapnel, two 24-pound howitzers amidships

H.M.S. Havannah, 19 gun fifth rate frigate, sail (originally 32 guns)

H.M.S. Hecate, 5 gun paddle wheel second class sloop, brigantine-rigged

H.M.S. Herald, 8 gun surveying vessel,

H.M.S. Inconstant, 36 gun fifth rate frigate (?)

Labouchere, H.B.C. paddle steamer

Louise, sloop

H.M.S. Monarch, 84 gun second-rate ship of the line, two 12-pound Howitzers, sail

Otter, H.B.C. propeller steamship, Brigantine-rigged, 4 brass cannons

H.M.S. Pandora, 4 gun packet brigantine-rigged, surveying ship

H.M.S. Pearl, 21 gun screw corvette

H.M.S. Pique, 36 gun fifth rate frigate

H.M.S. Plumper, 12 gun auxiliary steam survey sloop, barque-rigged, two long 32-pound guns, ten short 32-pound guns

H.M.S. Portland, 50 gun fourth rate frigate, flagship, Pacific Station, sail

H.M.S. President, 52 gun fourth rate frigate, sail

H.M.S. Pylades, 21 gun screw corvette

H.M.S. Satellite, 21 gun screw corvette

H.M.S. Scout, 21 gun screw corvette

H.M.S. Scylla, 21 gun screw corvette

H.M.S. Sparrowhawk, 4 gun screw gun vessel

H.M.S. Sutlej, 50 gun fourth rate screw frigate, Pacific flagship, including 35 heavy guns (twenty-two 68-pounders and four 110-pound Armstrong guns on the main deck, and eight 40-pound Armstrong guns and one 110-pound pivot gun on the forecastle)

H.M.S. Termagant, 25 gun screw frigate

H.M.S. Thetis, 36 gun fifth-rate frigate, sail

H.M.S. Topaze, 51 gun screw frigate

H.M.S. Tribune, 31 gun screw frigate

H.M.S. Trincomalee, 24 gun sixth-rate sailing frigate, including fourteen 32-pound guns

H.M.S. Virago, 6 gun paddle wheel first class sloop of war

H.M.S. Zealous, 20 gun screw central battery ironclad, flagship, Pacific Station

Dislodging: The Colonial Temperament at Cowichan Bay, circa 1900

To be a good counter-jumper, you must not only be able to sell folks things they want but things they don't want. I never could bring myself to do that. It was bad enough handing out goods you knew were shoddy at twice their value. I see myself helping a poor Indian into a grotesque suit and assuring him: 'It feet you like ze paper on ze vall.' Or selling a squaw a pair of shoes you knew were resistant as cardboard.

I hated myself for doing these things. I was never tainted with sordid commercialism. If I had been obliged to sell my own books, I would have died in the gutter. If revulsion to business is a sign of the artistic temperament, then I must really be an artist. Yet at the job of petty huckstering, though I hated it, I carried on for four years. The reason is that I was at a new low as regards morale. Spiritually I was bruised, if not broken. Any haven was a heaven. Here I was, rather under than over worked. I was warm, well fed, dry. I was looked on by the family as one of themselves. Consideration by people of my own class was not wasted on me, and gratitude for that kindness made me prolong my stay from year to year. I had been handled harshly by the world, and taking up the struggle affrighted me. So I continued to follow lethargically the lovely line of least resistance.

> Robert Service, 'Storekeeper' in *Ploughman of the Moon: An Adventure into Memory* (1945)

Adjacent to the wooden bridge over the slough where spawning fish, it's said, would get stuck between cartwheel spokes, and a *hwunitum* could shoot at ducks all day as if he owned the place, a general store was thrown up to prey on a population unprepared for the haste or discipline of

Occupation. It began with warships, and a hunger for pre-emption. Hangings and 32-pounders set the tone, resistance went to ground. Into the grief of smallpox marched evangelists. 'The theory of the instincts,' observed Freud, 'is so to say our mythology.' Occupiers industrialized the

chuck, provisioned the Navy, tore up graves with ploughs. The 'Siwashes' were retooled as marks, becoming adjacent to themselves—a precondition for abstraction, servitude and citizenship—and extruded as consumers, shelling out *hiyu dolla* to a foreign lackey to lug home a tin with a likeness on it of what they once gave away. It cost just to tear it open. Is destiny lodged in a name? In his chaste confession, purged of dates and names, Service is a louche tormentor, angling disingenuously in the slough of our forgiveness. Hireling *and* squireling, leashed to privilege,

julienned by hypocritical self-loathing, his libido's channelled into the lucrative moral paralysis that underwrote the spoils and burdens of imperial adventure. The charge? To commodify the Siwash, cram them into coalmines and log sorts, set them to canning, dusting, bleaching the

Bishop's underwear. In theory, service. In practice, supination. But after the necktie parties they got uppity. Rather give you the finger than lift one. We'll see when hard times come. Hired to humiliate the Hul'q'umi'num', the man who'll become the Canadian Kipling—a poem appeared in

the *Duncan Enterprise & Vancouver Island Advertiser* in 1903; another, 'Apart and Together', in *Munsey's Magazine*—appropriates his customers' only refuge, their abjection, claiming he was 'spiritually … bruised, if not broken' or, as he later puts it, 'sore as a boil.' He bullies a 'fat

klootchman' and her 'Buck', and hates himself. A man divided is the perfect pathogen. He costs the public nothing and spreads misery as by-products of his shame and self-evisceration. I'm grateful for his candour. Who'd not warm to such a civilized psychosis? And who, in his shoes,

would not leap at the Sunday chukka, the strings of trout, the cross-dressing theatricals in town? Self-reproach likes footlights. One hot August afternoon, high above the dozing sea—this is my inheritance—a young gentleman, fancying himself one of the 'men that don't fit in,' climbs a hill

without an English name to nap beneath a school of cloud sturgeon. Soon it's his hill ('mine to frame my Odyssey'); much later, he'll make a killing. In 1904, about the time Sidney Reilly, in a dog collar, was twisting William Knox D'Arcy's arm for the Anglo-Persian oil fields on a yacht

parked down the coast from Service's future home on the Riviera, the Cowichan 'cow-juice jerker' overcame his ennui and pulled the plug on under the counter booze. He lost his customers and his job. The double life? He taught school, became a teller, was sent to Kamloops, more polo, then Whitehorse, then fame. He suffered an eight-month infestation of boils in France while working for the Ambulance Corps in 1916, the year his brother was killed. 'My stretcher is one scarlet stain,' he wrote in *Rhymes of a Red Cross Man*, a set of jumpy, heartbreaking, dramatic

monologues in working-class dialects that lacked the High Church humility to breach the canon, nods to God in the final couplets notwithstanding. An eruption of boils on his back in the 1930s required surgical excision. A Cowichan named Shashia, or Tsosieten, who armed his men to

ambush northerners at Maple Bay in 1840, is said to have lost a son to a lanced boil. A poetics of boils in the theatre of human immanence is overdue. And too an analysis of shame, disgrace and sublimation among returned servicemen such as my grandfather after 1918. You'll find the

saddest sexual history the world has known. Is success a grave or a dory? Service sang on, often recklessly, as if determined to surprise or exhaust language, longing for a 'virgin vastitude' unstained by the linguistic order, which was difficult to distinguish from a marching order. Yet,

like 'Erbert 'Iggins, for whom '... *when it's most real, / It's then that you feel / You're a-watchin' a cinema show*,' Service was his own snare. Who isn't? I summon *H.M.C.S. Magnificent*, sailing into Halifax Harbour on a winter morning, all beaten gold. 'Instincts,' wrote Freud, 'are mythical beings,

magnificent in their elusiveness.' Karl Brandt, Hitler's doctor, described the Führer as being devoted to his mother who, he claimed, was an ocean of sobriety and humility. 'How unhappy my Mother would have been could she have seen her son in this position and with this responsibility,'

Brandt has Hitler muse. And Freud: 'In our work we cannot for a moment disregard them, yet we are never sure that we are seeing them clearly.' 'Mum, Mum, the *Maggie*!' In flight from mythical beings my mother spent the weeks between the Munich Agreement and the Molotov-Ribbentrop

Pact filling seed packets in the old general store, riding her bike to work. Service was in the USSR. Did he meet Tom McEwen? My mother has no memory of Cowichans, although the reserve was next door. She remembers women in the ditches, picking wool off barbed wire.

Forerunner (I)

A hairy man
loose head
loose mouth raving
twigs, skins, pips in the beard
spittle and bad teeth
asking, 'You work around here?'

A Messiah?

A skewer
jammed through the ribs
into my lung
and out again,
a guy too busy talking
to notice a tick
in his groin,
who leaves his engine
running,
his head
on a dish,
my name
at the door.

J'ai baisé ta bouche Iokanaan,
J'ai baisé ta bouche.

Forerunner (II)

hairy flaps
fore and aft
crossed a river
no one laughed

heard voices
in the sky
sang a psalm
chewed a fly

pushed his cousin
underwater
lost his head
to Herodias' daughter

listen: marching
in the east
armies of
St. Jean Baptiste

right behind
him, can't you see
the eternity
he tore from me?

At the Metropolitan Hotel

It was the elevator moaning.

Story of Origin

How she by train was
bundled
over the hills
village by village, south
to her father's side

again and again.

She'd sit on a stone wall
shouting to passing lorries,
'My mother's ninety-nine!'

She'd a rubber doll named Billy,
and because she wasn't the sort
to dress up dolls,
in fact,
didn't like dolls,
was surprised to find herself sobbing
after abandoning him one afternoon
on the wall.
Her mother hurried out at dawn.
No Billy.
A week later there he was,
straddling the cannon
of a tank
on high street,
starkers.

One morning the field behind them
swarmed with soldiers.
Her mother ran outside.
Where're you from?
Canada, he said.

Nanaimo, he said.
I know it, she said.
What street?
I know it, she said.
What house? What house?
That was our house, she said,
our house,
to the bewildered islander
from the sky.

Booth Bay

Scales, quilts, clams, red roof, salal berries, hoes, hay for sale, sailing, sealing our shadow in, it was the summer after the war they loaded what was theirs onto a barge and towed it up the narrows through the rips and kingfishers to Booth Bay, here are the first snapshots, the roof needing gutters, the porch, dogs, lambs, lamps, tables and the returned—if that's a name for them—lighting beach fires, turning a field over into furrows, carrot rows, and their lovers, elbows and knees, hollow-eyed, fearful, sleepless, planting petunias in a little dugout canoe. But you're not dead, no matter how much you think that might have been easier, so you summoned the years, summoned your furious husband with his ripped-open forearm, barged it all up here where the summer hay and the tides dissolve definition, where sweet and tidal flow into one another and the heron puts down in the sea asparagus at dawn. You spent years searching out love's limits and did not come close.

One must be willing to cause harm.

You are fifty, it is 1946 and you perch on the porch rail with a cigarette pretending to look out at the bay. The shutter opens and closes. Living is dismembering. You will play it safe, you will switch to knowing. It will seem, to all of us, a gift.

Masquerade

the crow next door is certainly a fox terrier
nothing on earth is ever
satisfied or dear
to itself

that said,
nice grub presentation

The Post Road

It is difficult not to be fictitious in so fair a place ...
                                        Emily Dickinson

Her bedroom an ear, a spine of resistance, a machine for tuning herself to the universe. At night, in deep snow, with curtains drawn, the household asleep, journeying outward into deviation and blasphemy—and majesty, and, by God, *arriving*. Swinging a lantern at the magnolia routs my

fourteen thousand six hundred and seven days of snickering indignation and entitlement glazed with disingenuous Thumperismo. Blanket proxies. That you won't find my fingerprints anywhere they shouldn't be is a measure of my failure. The letters, she discovers—no, the sounds of them—

sit precisely one over the other. The tainted letters on top, the capes, she disables at her desk each night and reconfigures in a fierce, shamanic concentration of will. It takes everything she has. Why is she not out squeezing money from the pious to school distant heathens in kneeling, petit

point and 'Breathe on me, breath of God'? Because in that ordinary upstairs bedroom on certain nights, in a halo of fiery coal oil, verbs *verb*, thunder *thunders*, God *Gods* in clear sight of the Amherst post road. If the guide sexing her up only knew. She is the eye of the filleting knife, the

agate a bride reaches for on a New Bedford shore, she is Melville's *NO! in thunder*. No, she did not sit still; how could she? Why would she when the gates of Eternity burst open like the tail of a thrashing fish? Write an elegy? How could she? Death does not die. I could not take my eyes off

the oak. I'm wondering if Ben Heppner will sing the Italian tenor's aria in next year's *Rosenkavalier*. The Trustees have spread hog fuel beneath the hickories. The path wide enough for two we saved for last. In harem trousers at Walden Pond, in skirts turned inside out, with ear trumpets and

sticks, the wicked, the sick, the weak minded—the marks—blaze through the heaving pines. It's all she can do to pull back the hammer, load the words, then there's the baking and that magnolia on the east lawn is pushy, it's dawn already, the earth has moved, her syllables are, then hell

breaks loose, sun *suns*, leaves *leaf,* she *shes*—she's *sheing!* Heart pounding, can't breathe, she's *whirling, burning*—a wheel of tansy in a hurricane. Yes, her hem stroked the Indian Pipes where love forgot itself for *athanasia*, but what business is it of yours? You say you fear death? Try life.

Bedford Basin

the wounds I fled
the red and yellow
coils of dynamite wire
my hand was the drum for

men calling in the night
flashlights
the shout of water
on the hill

my mother's tears
faces torn and glued to one another
a pot on stones boiling
a girl with a snake in her shirt.

Reading for Dummies

The room must be dark with a pillar of light
emerging from the page. The table is set at the far end
of a tea room in a busy railway station
in a foreign capital. The choir is dismissed.
The act consumes you.

The passenger in 33E

'Do you know the little stream?' she asks.
Something ancient rolls over and smiles.

May I take you, falling man, into my arms?
Falling daughter, falling mother,
may I rest here
in your arms?

The incident, referred to by veterans as 'the world is a pool of liquefied shite,' occurred in a lonely drinking club above an abandoned biological testing lab haunted by unwanted mariners and, briefly, by a table of ambitious poets, journalists and would-be Lowrys who relished the kitschy gimbal hoods and oar altars of the proprietor whose father, a stoker, had perished in the furnaces of the *Empress of China* on her maiden voyage. 'Night,' they began in unison, 'is a dark trawler.'

Eye mite?

I might.

Flying Bird Pen

'It Appears To the Life While Write'

Roland Barthes in the Kootenays

I'd like to thank Pauline Butling and the organisers of this historic gathering for inviting me to speak today as part of a panel entitled 'Faking It.' At first I thought I would talk about poetry and documentary. Fred Wah and I had a lively conversation about documentary some years back, and I often think about that conversation and about how I've wanted to return to it in reference to his writing and to the writing of his generation. It fits in with some work I'm doing at the moment. But, by chance, I received a letter last week, and it concerned something, a series of unusual events, I haven't been able to speak about for some years, ever, really, and now, I think, given the circumstances, it's probably permissible to say a few words. I guess it shouldn't surprise me that this remarkable conference brings with it a kind of serendipity. For what I'm about to tell you is something I've had to keep to myself for over twenty years. It seems like a dream now. But it's because of his fierce resistance to biography, all through his life, and his conviction that the anecdotal is little more than an indulgence of the delusional I, that I've respected his wishes and kept silent. I'm speaking of, well, I should, I should just go back to the beginning.

I was teaching for a year in the East Kootenays of British Columbia, in Cranbrook, a small, self-conscious city made famous by Oliver Sacks. It was late 1979, and I didn't know Fred at that time. I was teaching undergraduate English at the local college and had stacks of papers to mark every night. Late one afternoon I received a phone call. It was from a person in Toronto I didn't know, a representative of the Toronto Semiological Circle, which, at that time, had a strong following at the University of Toronto. I don't know how they found my name. Perhaps it was from the professor at SFU who had recommended me for the job in Cranbrook where I was standing in for an instructor who was away in China for a year.

The voice introduced itself.

'Are you free this evening?' it asked, tentative.

'It depends,' I replied.

There was a pause. 'It's rather crucial for us to know if you have any spare time in the next few hours,' the voice said.

I told him, yes, I had a few things I had to do, but ....

'It would really help us out if you could, you know ... we're in a pinch ....'

'Sure,' I said.

There was another pause. I heard some papers shuffling.

He asked, 'Are you familiar with the name Roland Barthes?'

I confessed I had come to Barthes' work belatedly. It was 1979, I certainly didn't know as much as I felt I should.

Then he whispered. 'You can't tell anybody about this. He's in British Columbia. We need your help.'

It turned out that—you probably know this already, and after almost a quarter of a century, I hope I've got the details correct—one of Barthes' great uncles, I think, had been an administrator with one of the railroad companies in France. And this man's younger cousin, who was equivalent in a way to Barthes' great aunt, was living at that time near Nakusp on the Arrow Lakes. For mysterious reasons her son had left France after the Second World War—I never did find out why—and had settled in the Interior of British Columbia.

After the son's wife died, his mother, by now a widow, had come out to British Columbia to live with him, and by the time I came into the picture she was very sick and frail and had contacted Barthes, asking him to visit her as soon as possible. He didn't tell me, naturally enough, why he had to see her so urgently, or even, in fact, why he was in Canada. It was none of my business. But, in any case, when the caller from Toronto told me this and mentioned the name Roland Barthes, what else could I say but, 'Of course.'

Then he asked, 'Do you know anything about the Castlegar airport?'

I remember being surprised to hear those oddly intimate syllables being formed in the mouth of a stranger.

'He's circling around in the air right now,' he said, 'somewhere above Castlegar.'

Some of you, I know, are aware of just how terrifying this can be. I'd had the experience more than once of doing doughnuts in impenetrable fog and cloud above that rocky, unforgiving landscape for what seemed to be an eternity. You understand in a sweaty, not entirely selfless way, that the pilot is trying to decide which course of action will allow him to save the greatest number of passengers' lives: to risk putting down at Castlegar, which depends on a merciful gust of wind ripping the clouds apart above the runway at the exact moment that the aircraft plunges to the ground, or to turn back to Penticton and risk slamming into the jagged limestone walls of the narrow canyon through which the aircraft is hurtling on its approach to the field. You grip the seat, feeling for the useless life jacket Velcroed underneath, waiting for the engines to accelerate, or decelerate, or cut out entirely; and then the limestone rock face appears, two or three feet off the end of the wingtip as you shudder by in the swirling fog and sleet ....

The voice said, 'It looks like he's not going to be able to land in Castlegar. The plane's been re-routed. Would you be willing to pick him up when he arrives in Cranbrook and get him to Nelson by tomorrow morning? He's on a tight schedule.'

'Of course.'

And then he repeated his warning. 'You must promise never to tell a soul.'

And I said that was all right with me.

So, I got into my car and drove out to the Cranbrook airport. There had been a terrible accident there, if you remember, a scheduled flight had plunged into the runway a few months earlier. I was already imagining the headlines: ROLAND BARTHES DIES IN FIERY CRASH AT CRANBROOK AIRPORT! The name might not have been featured so prominently in the Cranbrook *Daily Townsman*, but somewhere else it would have. And as I drove out past the little farms and the clumps of spindly larch, I wondered—how would I recognise him? How will I know it's him when I see Roland Barthes in the Cranbrook Airport? I got there early and I was waiting, I was marking student essays, and I guess I had become preoccupied with the novel contractions of that region because it was a surprise to find a shortish man suddenly standing before me wearing a grey suit and a clear plastic raincoat. I must have given him a startled look.

'For transparency,' he said, and smiled broadly.

There was still snow on the ground. It was cold, and he walked out in his, in the way he moved, he was short ... I don't know if any of you have met him, but he reminded me of a squirrel. And he possessed a vulnerable, otherworldly magnetism. I mean, I'd just met him and I was filled with an impulse to just hold him. Out we came, into the cold dusk, and we got into the car and we smiled, and it became apparent that he was truly rattled—terrified and exhausted—after his stuttering, heart-knocking flight through the snowbound mountains of British Columbia. We didn't say anything very much to begin with. I was, I think, a little overwhelmed. My French isn't great. I'd spoken it colloquially at St. Jean and had studied briefly, ineptly, with Gatien Lapointe—what an opportunity I'd wasted!—and so, eventually, we managed to exchange a few awkward sentence fragments as we drove through the twilight into town.

If you know the Cranbrook Airport, you'll remember that you must drive through an Indian Reserve to get to town and that you pass a splendid and imposing residential school on the way. I think it was called St. Mary's. The main residential school building resembles an abandoned movie set on the edge of Shangri-la; it must have been a source of unremitting misery for the kids who were incarcerated there. You come down a hill, turn a corner and there it is: an unexpectedly elegant and disturbing French chateau gazing out serenely at the western slope of the Rockies. There's a huge lawn in front of it and on a moonlit night it's a haunting, spectral sight.

Although it was cold and damp, the clouds had pulled apart and the moon was rising, and as we skidded around the corner on the muddy road he glanced over and caught sight of the school. Moonlight was reflecting off the walls and windows, and he was transfixed. I'd felt the enchantment too, when I first saw the building, and we drove toward it slowly and expectantly. Two long rows of Lombardy poplars line the driveway and we coasted down between them in silence. He sat motionless in the front seat. The school had been run by the Oblates, and so the atmosphere, if I may call it that, of discipline and intimidation, was familiar to him. We turned to face the mountains and sat there silently, gazing out the windows in the luminous night. I watched his face and thought to myself, 'Here I am, sitting in my old heap with Roland Barthes, hypnotised by the moon at St. Mary's.'

It was getting cold, but I didn't want to break the spell, and as we drove away I decided not to turn my car's headlights on. George Bowering will remember that this is a habit of mine on a moonlit night. I hate to have the headlights on, especially when travelling through the mountains.

We drove all the way into Cranbrook without headlights. In those days you had to switch the lights on yourself. It was marvellous, cruising through the snowy night by the light of the moon along a silver highway. We were both enchanted, despite the fact that Barthes was exhausted. (I apologise for checking my notes. I thought I'd forgotten some details when writing them out, but I'm remembering more, here, as I'm telling the story.) I had the impression that he'd not experienced this sort of familiar-to-us cultural dislocation before. He was unceasingly curious, however, although I'll just mention one or two examples.

He was, it turns out, very interested in tribal narratives and histories, not in any kind of mythological way but in structural terms, as you might imagine. And, at that time, I think you'd have to agree, French critics were what you might call potlatch opportunists. They believed that the potlatch represented an enlightened model of pre-industrial communism in action, and so coming to British Columbia presented a thrilling opportunity for Barthes; he was hoping he might somehow attend a potlatch. He was in the Kootenays for only thirty-six hours, and I was sorry that I had to disabuse him of the notion that he was coming to the land of the Ur-socialists. I think he thought he'd be able to drop into a local potlatch and there'd be masks and stories and blankets and dancing, who knows, maybe they'd know Levi-Strauss, or he'd meet his very own Kutenai Adario, you know, and it'd be, 'Oh hey, yeah, we remember Claude …!'

One of the things he was really curious about and, you must remember, this was the final year of his life—although, as you know, he died as a result of a car accident—he was getting on in years, he hadn't been well for much of his life, and one of the things he did talk about, I do remember, is a Melanesian custom whereby, when a person dies, the people in the band, or village, or whatever the group was, would drop certain words out of their vocabulary for a while during the period of grieving. He liked that idea very much; he was keen on formal funerary customs, and he held forth in this vein as we drove into the centre of town. He believed that human beings, if they willed it so, held their destinies in their own hands; that there was nothing, collectively, we could not achieve if we put our minds to it. He believed in the Revolution, although in the East Kootenays it was hardly a hot topic. And one thing, I've never forgotten it, he cited Trotsky—although now I'm not sure whether it was Trotsky or Lenin—he said, 'You know, if the sun is bourgeois we will stop the sun.' We were talking about death and dying and words that were lost, and as we waited at the traffic lights near the Tamarack Mall, he turned to me and said, soulfully, 'You know, the socialist project should be able to stop death.'

It seems startling to repeat these words today, but it was still possible then to share in the collective dream of liberation, to believe that our ideas were charged with a kind of primal inevitability, to experience in our hearts the uplifting optimism of the will we all talked about. It was 1979. He turned to me as we pulled into the driveway and said, 'If death is bourgeois we will even stop death,' and he meant it, shaking his tiny squirrel fist in the air.

We entered the house. It was a recently built rancher in Cranbrook. I showed Barthes to his bedroom. He opened his suitcase and the top layer consisted entirely of medications. Pills, bottles with droppers, and all sorts of things in boxes and jars, and I didn't really want to stare, but how could I help it? With a solemn ceremony, with a small, precise ceremony, he soon began tilting his head back and swallowing the pills. He'd been up for hours, of course, as you can imagine, I'm sure, and, I mean, he was an old man so I wanted to leave him alone, but there, lying beneath the pills on top of his shirts, lying on top of his precisely folded shirts in preparation for being in British Columbia, I couldn't help noticing, was a well-read copy of Fred Wah's *Pictograms from the Interior of B.C.*

I'll tell you a little more about this in a minute. Now, I had no food in the house, and when I mentioned this he looked up and said, in French, something like, 'Why would we choose to eat here?' I figure I can make an omelette with the best of them, but, as it was late, we decided to go out to a restaurant which some of us at the college frequented in those days. It was run by a young family from the PRC—recently arrived—and somebody had sent them out to Cranbrook, and here they were, struggling to make great meals and to entice new customers, but few Cranbrookians, a naturally suspicious lot, darkened their door. A Chinese family. They couldn't speak English very well, and I liked them a lot. The food was fresh and tasty, and I suppose, in our own peculiar ways, we were all exiles there, and so I had become a regular.

The restaurant was on the ground floor of a crumbling brick building no one paid much attention to. In the old days, when Cranbrook was filled with miners, it would have been in the heart of its now dismantled Chinatown. It would also have been at the centre of the city's red light district. I was telling Barthes about this phantom world, and he was really quite excited to discover that we were dining in what had once been the city's 'zone of transgression.' I mentioned to him how, years ago, the city fathers—and this is a notorious event in Cranbrook's history—the city fathers, in a misplaced but popular and mean-spirited, hypocritical exercise of their authority, had evicted the prostitutes from their cosy premises and marched them up the main street as a way of shaming and, I suppose, disowning them. At a movie club screening I'd met an old timer who, as a young boy, had experienced an epiphany while watching the bedraggled parade of women through the windows of his high school classroom. The courage of this defiant group of women had made a profound impression on him, and he found himself respecting them more than he respected his own righteous parents. The women were driven through the cold rain that day to the Cranbrook city dump where they were forced to live in tents.

I told this story to Barthes and he said, 'Let's do it!'

'What do you mean?'

'In solidarity with those women,' he declared, 'we should honour that march.'

And so after dinner that's what we did, we walked up Baker Street. We went on that march. Not as far as the dump. (I should tell you that a few years later the new community college was built on that dump site.) But we did march up as far as the Safeway. There I'd been, not even four hours earlier, thinking, 'God, only thirty-eight more papers to mark,' and now here I was marching along Baker Street with Roland Barthes and we were staring at the moon and it was a freezing cold night, and we went into the Safeway, and as we were picking out our shopping baskets he was talking a mile a minute, in French, and he looked at me suddenly and asked, 'Do you know this book, *Pictograms from the Interior of B.C.*?'

'I do,' I said. 'It's an extraordinary book.'

'I've never seen anything like it,' he said.

Fred, I told him, was a poet I admired, and then he looked at me again.

'I brought it with me,' he said, 'this book.'

'I saw it in your suitcase,' I said. I was wondering how he'd ever managed to find a copy.

He'd discovered it at La Hune on St. Germain in Paris; he'd found a copy there and had brought it to Canada with him. And what excited him is that he, he'd read it, and someone had told him, or he'd found out somehow that *Pictograms* was not a translation. This is what thrilled him the most.

'At last,' he said, 'we've overcome the obsession with translation.'

He took this very seriously.

And he kept asking me, 'Fred Wah, he's an Indian?'

No, I said.

But that name—Fred WAH?'

I said, 'No, don't say it that way. He's not an Indian, or an aboriginal person at all.'

If he was disappointed he didn't say anything. It made no difference in the end to his appreciation of Fred's text. *Pictograms* had opened up new possibilities, and because it had made such an impression on him Barthes was certain that everybody in British Columbia would be familiar with the book.

We began rolling our cart through the Safeway and he was, I should tell you, he was as fond of smoking, of the act of smoking, as anyone I've ever met. I mean, he'd had tuberculosis, and yet here we were going in for a carton of cigarettes. And he wanted to explore, to take the measure of a Canadian *hypermarché*. I was looking for some juice for the morning, and perhaps some croissants, and he was examining things, he was looking at signs and colours and pointing out this and that and before I knew it he was talking about Fred's book to a young guy with a crew cut piling up oranges in the produce section. The boy was nodding vigorously, politely.

I heard the words '... revolutionary text,' then Barthes gave me a sharp look.

The boy looked up at Roland Barthes and said—I'm trying to remember exactly what he said—it was something between a snort and a gasp—the boy stared at him, and Barthes began, very patiently I thought, to explain in detail what he meant by Fred's non-allegorical enunciative practice, including something astonishingly, piercingly relevant about the opening image, and, finally—the boy's just standing there with his mouth open, gobsmacked—Barthes gulps for breath, he's so excited to be, you know, here, and declares, explosively, stamping his foot, 'This little book, at last ...,' he hesitated while he found the exact words in English, 'you must see, he has freed us from the mythological nausea!' I'll never forget the worried look on the young man's face.

Barthes spun around and declared, 'I want to see more,' and off he went. Now, mysteriously, in this Safeway at the end of Baker Street, there was in the centre aisle a big metal wire basket stuffed with remaindered books. No, it's not going to be that; *The Fashion System* was not among them. But while Barthes was examining the Jell-O packages and the vegetables, I began rooting around in the basket—who of us can stop ourselves when the opportunity arises—and I found a flawless first American edition of Thomas Bernhard's *Correction* in English. I don't know if you know this extraordinary novel—it more or less feels like one long paragraph, one long prickly sentence—marked down to $4.99. There, at Safeway, in Cranbrook. I can't tell you if there are any left; it's long drive, it may be worth a phone call ....

In any case, Barthes was suddenly at my side and he stared at the book in my hand. I said, rather feebly, 'Thomas Bernhard.'

'I know,' he said. 'Where did you find it?'

I could see that he was revising his opinion of the literary maturity of Cranbrook and western Canada in general.

I gestured to the remainder bin. It felt as if a strange and troubling surge of mimetic rivalry had ambushed and overtaken us. I wasn't sure what to do. I could sense that he wanted it, the copy, a copy of this translation of the Bernhard. At the same time, I wanted it. I hadn't spotted it anywhere else in town, or in the entire country for that matter. And then I began thinking, 'My God, I'm getting competitive with Roland Barthes over a book. He's here for 36 hours, he's an old man, one of the giants of the twentieth century, and I'm saying you can't have this $4.99 remaindered novel. Surely I can find it again, you know, somewhere else ....' And then, before I knew it, he was waist deep in the book basket, head buried, trouser cuffs kicking in the air, snuffling a little, like a passenger on a sinking ship digging for the last life jacket.

He found a copy; thank God he found a copy. And so it was with some smugness, having straightened out our clothes, that both of us proceeded to the cash, picking up a carton of Rothman's on the way, to purchase the two remaining copies of *Correction* in Cranbrook, B.C., or in entire world for all we knew.

When we got back to the house he went right to bed; there was no further talk. The next morning we had to leave early as the woman who was going to meet him in Nelson would be waiting. And so off we went in the early morning darkness, and we managed to get over the Salmo-Creston pass without any kind of incident. He slept most of the way. He woke up at one point, just after dawn, as we crested the summit. I should have mentioned before that he'd recently, I think, become enthusiastic about Sir Philip Sidney's *The Defence of Poesie*. He woke up suddenly, gazed about him at the snowdrifts, rubbed his eyes, turned to me and asked, plaintively, '*Fugientem haec terra videbit?*'

'Shall this land see me a fugitive?'

He launched into a heady, impromptu analysis of Sidney's manifesto in French and in English. It's startling now to recall this exhilarating moment in my old black Volvo, slithering through the Purcells. Barthes explained that while he had an abiding enthusiasm for Sidney's enthusiasm, he was otherwise appalled by his inadequate argument. That such enthusiasm could be inspired and sustained by ideas that were so misplaced intrigued him. He felt that this was an almost exclusively English ability, although I thought that perhaps he was testing this theory by asking me some probing questions about writing in English-speaking Canada. In any case, he felt that if only Sidney had been able to dispense with his ludicrous, delusional argument he might have written the perfect book—because of the enthusiasm, because of the absolute, the intuitively muscular flow of the text. I can't remember any other details; that's more or less the gist of what he said. He fell asleep again soon after, en route to Yahk.

I'd promised him the evening before that I would try to take him to visit Fred. He'd asked if he might meet the man who had written *Pictograms from the Interior of B.C.*, and I said he lives not too far away, as far as I knew. So, playing hooky, we zipped through Nelson and out to South Slocan. It's only a few miles the other side. Barthes had dozed off again. He was slumped beside me, and I didn't know at that time where Pauline and Fred were living, so I stopped and asked, and found out where their house was.

We wound our way up the driveway and I think he still imagined or hoped that he might see a tepee, or a pit house—a *kekuli* house. It looked like no one was home. I went up and knocked on the door. Barthes stayed in the car. I knocked on all the doors. I knocked on and peeked through the windows of the house I was later so very happy to live in, but not a soul was present. So I walked back to the car and said, to a dejected Roland Barthes, 'No one's home. I'm very sorry.' I looked at my watch and it was time for us to get back to Nelson.

Fred, I'm sorry. I tried.

It began to snow as we rushed back into town. I gave him into the hands of the woman in Nelson and he disappeared. I never saw him again. The suddenness of his departure surprised me and left me feeling sad and bereft. I hadn't expected to enjoy such companionship, or that I would miss it so. That's all I can say, really. I've reported to you, as faithfully as I am able to, our conversations. I think the only thing I should add is that, from what I could see, he was disinterested in the exemplary. He was not pursued by the belief that one must strive for an exemplary life. In fact, I'd say he was enthusiastically devoted to demolishing the idea of the exemplary life in favour of something more fragile and momentary. Daily existence, I think, for him, had to do with the projection of one's subjectivity onto another. Life could be lived passionately only in the fugitive, disintegrating, blessed moments when one was neither oneself nor the other. His absorption in the endearing gestures of legible signage, wearied by recurrence, was, I'm almost certain, driven by his desire to plunge somehow, as a sentient creature, beyond the circumferences of history, geography and time.

I'm extrapolating, perhaps, on that last bit, but, in any case, there you have it: my scrape with Roland Barthes. I just have to say once again that he had such great respect for Fred's book. He really saw it for what it is. At one point he exclaimed, 'This book draws a line between everything that comes after it, and the century that preceded it.'

That's it. I think I mentioned when I began that I was not permitted to speak about this matter before now because of Barthes' desire for privacy and his absolute resistance to the performance of biography, but there is, I'm told, a much anticipated memoir coming out next year. So I'm sure it's fine, at least as much as I've told you. I have not betrayed any confidences by reporting on some of the literary aspects of Roland Barthes' lightning visit to the East and West Kootenays almost twenty-five years ago. It meant a great deal to me, as you might imagine, as an impatient young man, but, more to the point, it's something I've had a terrible time keeping from Fred for all these years. So, there you are; and thank you Fred, and thank you all for listening.

Half-Measures

for Susanna Browne

If I were a bird, no, that's been said;
if I were a gull, or a bell, oh damn! If I were a ship
or a plum or a shed or a tree or a star or a clam …?
If I were a spire in Malta, or maybe Gibraltar,
and were hit by a nasty typhoon,
would I be a defaulter on the way to the altar,
would I storm down the aisle with a lunatic smile,
love's latest buffoon?

I once dreamed of chalk and a starting line
and a referee with a little black gun.
But now that I'm here the view's not (nearly) so clear.
Where to begin? Have I begun?
I thought this was supposed to be fun.

In the news there's no end to calamity.
Our turn's just a matter of time, so it seems.
My Dad sends money to Amnesty, he lives
in a fantasy, I seem to survive on dreams.
I want loves that explode and regiments clashing,
cymbals clanging and lightning flashing
in a mighty crescendo without innuendo, without any endo,
as putti tilt in on their wings.

I once dreamed of a pond with amphibians,
and myself in a little black dress;
But since I got here, all they do is drink beer,
they tell me to settle for less.
Who's paying, and what's her address?

On the corner I wait for the light to turn green,
staring at something pink. There's a boy
I like, and he likes me I think, but he's not really

looking at me. I don't know why we all dote
on our nation; a nation's an ocean
of woe. 'Just who must I serve?' is
my question, and who profits from my libido?
And anyway, who wants to know?

I once dreamed of justice and harmony,
and a garden sans clippers or hedgers.
Now I fill out the form, but I pray for the storm;
how I despise half-measures.
Why should I hide my treasures?

Half-measures are the Tora Bora of the tyrant,
the bully-boy, the whiner, the lonesome piner in the gloom.
Give me salt and fat and bravery to withstand
the army and the knavery of those who try to
seal me in my tomb. I'm the horse, I'm the track,
so take your god, don't bring him back. He's a
coward, he's a crank, he's always pulling rank.
Hey you, the ship of fools just sank.

I once dreamed of the scent of magnolia,
and tangos drawn out at our leisure.
But I'm nobody's tootsie, I refuse to play footsie
with the hawkers of half-measures,
with the fools who are tools of the ledgers.

My love is ambitious, it doesn't do dishes.
O how I hate half-measures.
O how I fear half measures.

A Rotary Ricer

for Robin Blaser

'… *più angusto vaglio* …'

Imagine a ricer, a rotary ricer, what could be nicer than taking a spin in its swirls?
Its whorls are worlds are the rings he sings, the circles he sifts with a 'finer sieve',
with a lover's ferocity, in major and minor key.

From within, the punctures in the tin are stars; they pierce celestial cinemas.
That's what, on a Maundy Thursday, a magnolia does to the air.
From his eyrie he can see two blooming there.

I heard a girl beside a bus repeat, '*Orphée, respiro.*' Poet, sing *we* into
the world. Sing the sweet and salty men, the men with broken knees
hanging in magnolia trees: '… *e vidi Orfeo.*'

Orbiting, orbiting, we're in the spin the pestle's in,
ricing, dicing, cutting it thin,
squeezing, extracting, distilling, compacting—
our garden's a desert without tears—
how thick and sweet the syrup
after eighty years.

Who dares to remember? Who dares to praise?
Who dares, these days?

Our beloved, in the
furnace of his ways.
Our hearts in his safekeeping,
our words in his safekeeping,
our rage in his safekeeping,
our love in his safekeeping,
our hearts, our words, our rage, our love
in his safekeeping.

Log Sort

'This
is where we sat,' says my Mum,
out of what's called the blue, to three young
strangers sitting at her table, dipping fries. 'Long ago, with
Marge and J.B.' She picks a poppy seed off her bun, gazing at stacks
of lumber across   Cowichan Bay. I propose   a class-analysis
of failing resorts. She is exhausted from the bun. Last fall when we drove out for
lunch at the motel beside the new Tim Horton's she watched the hockey game. I
drew on the placemat a plate of bacon and two eggs which, upside down, she
saw as a face. She pulled it from me,
took my pen,
and on the cheeks below the egg eyes
drew chains of tears.
'Where do you live?'
she asked.

The Shovel

for H.B.

The book is a shovel. It buries everyone. Buckram our pall, our ossuary, our unyielding second front. A ship stands by, the *Milky Way*. We should be so lucky. Not far from here, along hallucinating grades that skirt or seal the industrial school's unmarked graves, an old man will tell

you this beach is where a half-buried log lifted its throat out of the sand. He may or may not tell you this is where the first man and his wife stepped lightly out from between two fallen trunks. Here, in their metal beds, children lay rigid, listening for the shovel in the night. Eden and hell, in

step. The book is a shovel, a D8 blade, an admission of failure, a dare, an arc of spectral purity sealing the circumference of a boundless sphere above a trench of glimmering coals. The book shoves you out the door; it pushes you down the stairs, and with flywheels and pistons, cogs, rails,

capacitors and the turbulent majesty of sparks it consumes the weeping burning world only your body—*with you in it*—can complete. If you come at night to the bank of the river that pours between a melody and its likeness you'll be torn in two. You'll discover that you're already torn in

two. Will you ever be happy again? Not in the way you were. It will be as if you're suspended above a screaming sawmill. Sentries with peevees will strike from below until you fall, or until you grasp the shovel and enlist. Then the shining, intricate machinery will be yours. You'll take up

your Jerusalem and carry it with you. Even if it's not yours, it's yours. Heaven, from a haft. You'll portage your dead. You'll copulate recklessly on the ancient mounds while thieves strip corpses for curios. The book will bear you, bind you, name you. You'll become Sun, wrathful and fiery.

The book is a furnace. You'll incinerate continents. Anthems and prophecies will sustain you. Ambitious strangers will embrace you. One of those strangers may be your ruined father. I fought mine with arrogant fancies and cheap shots, carping and capering, hot to draw blood. What can

he have thought of his ignorant son with the little red etherizing book? Who cared? Not the gleeful sloganeer. I abandoned my father. Cowardice and complacency put God off; I went evangelizing. When I awoke it was dark, my wallet was gone. The shovel is God's bier. Rejoice,

The Heights

for Karl Siegler

Maintenance at the haemorrhoidal right turn of life is a volcano of self-bamboozlement. I've got Marching Mothers on at a modest reduction for a limited time. The girls sang bravely in the fervid antique way of torched muslin. I've brought the green trousers, a little stained but, let's

face it, too often the circle's not vicious enough. My friend called Sunday to say we missed the stars. But they were in my eyes. Everyone's griping; 'What we need now ….' I'm sceptical. What do they mean by 'now'? I worked with Dick Cheney for a little over a year when we were both a

lot younger; a straighter arrow you won't find. I loved the guy. Should I lie? He may not be able to tell you the number of days a katsura takes to leaf but how often would I be drifting home late from the Institute with Corporal Lemieux at the wheel—I'll never forget those orchid-scented

nights—the orange phone would ring, she'd turn, '*C'est pour vous, Monsieur Lebrun,*' and it'd be Dick, at his desk, with a whole new read. I know. I could say, 'If only you'd known him then,' but we hardly knew ourselves. In those days we were just connecting the dots. I mean, for us it was sport,

a rush, and we had access to firepower. I don't mean a few dysfunctional Dumbos lumbering over the Alps. We had a fix on those who troubled our sleep. What would begin as a laugh in our little cubby on the fifth floor, slicing up pizza with a Mastercard—Mozzaland here, Pepperonistan

there—produced real pain. You don't put something like that behind you without regret. There were, I'll admit, a few low months. But you can't shed a tear for someone who snapped an ankle in his own hole. Talk to a racehorse. When the PMO rang I told them to get serious. Who likes a

demotion? I held out. But everyone's got his sad little price. What sold me on the poetics portfolio was the chance to reconnect with the big leagues. Aim low, sink lower. Not that every assignment was a peach. I'd spend days pumping out acrostics for the Deputy: 'Al's little poetry utopia ruined

Dorothy's youth,' etc. There were highlights: Margaret Hollingsworth striding into a den of cut-throats in Pimlico; an afternoon in the Kunming bird market with Fred Wah, freeing sparrows when backs were turned; rattling through Al-Rajajil on an arthritic she-camel with John Newlove, caught near Jericho. Neither of us was eager to leave that sanctuary. Two hours later, after a stop at the British war cemetery in Jerusalem to say a prayer for my great uncle Percy, lugged through the Jaffa Gate on a cart at the frayed end of General Allenby's column, we were accelerating past

Jericho on our way north. Uncle Percy was felled, apparently, by a Turkish bullet, which was the kindest dispatch. Most soldiers in the Middle East in 1917 died from infections, heatstroke or chronic, bowel-gutting, body-spurting dysentery, dying in mushy heaps along the riverbanks.

Derrida was thoughtful. I'd discovered that he'd planned to attend a conference with my Québec counterpart and when she'd become ill the Department, unaware and in a panic, sent me as her replacement. He seemed to be disappointed. We drove up the doleful valley with its thin-wristed

boys holding out wilted vegetables to passing cars. Shredded plastic swirled in the fields. Derrida had met Sophie at a semiotic circle in Toronto. Their friendship was platonic, but they'd experienced an undeniable attraction, a kinship each likened to finding a lost sibling. Drawn from

opposite sides of the ocean, they shared the passionate, almost mystical conviction that one might complete the other. Sophie's family was Moroccan; like Derrida she was an amateur scholar of the Zohar. They'd decided to travel together to Safed, in part for reasons of shared scholarship,

and, risking catastrophe—or apostrophe—to spend time in one another's company. What might they discover? Would it be like entering a newly discovered text and finding it as familiar as the cyst in your hand? Perhaps Derrida was relieved by my arrival; I think he felt he was not able to

trust his heart, which was generous, impulsive and passionate. Twice he pulled out a photograph of an intense, dark-haired woman I recognized as my boss. I was clearly redundant, so we decided I'd drop him in Safed to carry on with some independent study, and as I had a few days to kill I'd

return to Jerusalem—the tomb of life, he called it—to commune with great uncle Percy, perhaps hike out into the wilderness. It was a shock when the Galilee appeared before us. Derrida asked if I'd be willing to make a detour to the ruins of Sussita or, as the Greeks knew it, Antiochia Hippos, or just Hippos—the horse—on the old road from Damascus to the sea. The sun was hot. Our little car whined up the switchbacks through rock and scrub toward the primal savannah of the Golan Heights. To stand upright and alone on that plateau, in a sea of grass, in a hard wind,

beside a forgotten dolmen, is to experience the existential terror of the Iron Age hunter. I parked on a scab of gravel at the side of the road. A handmade sign pointed to a narrow ridge camels once shuffled along on their way to a city of 20,000 glaring at its rival, Tiberias, across the blue

lake. Before I managed to smear on sunscreen and adjust my hat strap, my charge was dashing along the ridge with his jacket flapping in the wind, white hair streaming. He began to caper in an antic way, as if suspended by strings, waving his arms in wild semaphore. Picking my way along

the path, I noticed that both edges were lined with ramshackle wire fence. Metal signs with unfamiliar symbols clattered in the wind, harmonizing with rusty wires working themselves loose in little squeaks. He was breathing heavily. '*Des mines*,' he said, '*des mines dormantes*,' and he put his

hand to his ear, cocking his head as if to ask me if I could hear them sighing in their sleep. A weak smile. The scree falling away on both sides of the ridge had been planted with mines over the years by Syrians and Israelis, and I found myself wondering, stupidly, why they hadn't been

removed. I confess we were hypnotized by what we saw, or rather, by what we could not see, as we perched on that windy ridge. About us, the ancient landscape pitched and rolled. Scrubby bushes flared in pockets. Vultures plummeted from the bluffs into wadis ripped from the hills.

Derrida and I stared at the porous ground dropping away beneath us, our fingers wrapped tightly around the top wires of the fence. I think we shared the same attraction, not to the peril the mines proposed, but to the idea the idea of mines was beginning to suggest. For—and I could see this

question dawning in Derrida's mind—who could say if there were land mines present at all? They constituted in the beholder a sort of present absence, or was it an absent presence? Entire lives might be conceived, idealized, experienced and eulogized in the belief that mines had been planted in this flinty soil, though there might not be a mine for miles! Why would nations go to the trouble and expense of seeding mines when they could, with equal or even greater success, simply sow the idea of mines? Derrida and I glanced at one another. We'd been in a light trance.

Far below we could spy the blue, harp-shaped lake glistening like an olive, and I recalled that a publisher with that name issued the series of which he was editor, and had been responsible for his most recent book. I turned around, and he was already on the far side of the wire. I called out,

but he veered down the hill, kicking up little puffs of fine sand and shells. He was laughing, and began to dart teeteringly but freely between the rocks. He danced a jig, grinning like a little boy, and gave me a look of triumph. Was he testing me? I watched him prancing and sprinting,

picking up shell casings. For Derrida, thought counted or flowered only when married to or executed as action. Without a physical manifestation, thought was unfit to be called thought; it was an empty flirtation, the resort of the coward. His crown a white flame, the philosopher

skittered to the rocky bottom of a wadi in a flurry of fine dust, twirled once and once again, almost lost his balance, gave out a war whoop, tossed his mane and, with a glance at his watch, lurched up the hillside toward the fence. About six feet away from me, still beaming, he sprang

forward with his right foot and as it touched the ground the earth gave a little beneath it. He froze. Then he swallowed hard. '*Ne bougez pas*,' I said, unnecessarily. Wedged between earth and sky, like a wisp of chaff, he made a tender gesture with his eyes, indicating that I should move

away, slowly. I shuffled forward, tentative, but he waved one of his hands—I thought of a seal's flipper—and growled impatiently. '*Allez, allez.*' The late afternoon sun burned into my cheeks. Above us the vultures of Gamla dove in choral loops. The Kinneret had turned a metallic blue.

Derrida was trying to relax his muscles, preparing himself for what would come. Across the lake I could just make out Capernaum, where Christ raised Jairus' daughter. The air was still. Derrida stared at me, weighing my intentions. He smiled. '*J'ai mon délai*,' he said. 'It's perfect, *non? Et toi?*'

Provoked by his fearlessness, or was it a dare—a deliberate application of voltage to the erotic confusions of immanence—I found myself wanting. I was uncertain. If I moved away from him, I'd be abandoning him; if he collapsed or lost his balance, I'd be blown to smithereens. He was

doubtless contemplating the ironies of his final deconstruction. Clearly he was prepared to choose his own time, whether or not I joined him. I stood by uselessly, recklessly, listening to the vultures wheeling above. Would I choose brotherhood, standing arm-in-arm in solidarity with one of the

ravishing minds of the twentieth century, or indecision and craven self-interest? Why should I be saved? A helicopter appeared from nowhere and with turbines roaring flew directly over us into the valley, banking to the right, making for Metulla and the tidy green hills of the border, so

evocative of the Okanagan. The chopper's rattle hung in the air, unnerving us both. Derrida gave me a puppyish look. For an instant I felt sorry for the man who until that moment had seemed so charmed, so invincibly the steel-shanked agent of his own destiny. He was plainly unaccustomed

to asking for sympathy which, let's face it, is a plea to be forgiven for self-inflicted stupidity. I had an idea. '*Restez-là, M. Derrida*,' I said, and made a dash for our little white car. It was a tin kiln. Happily the Jack Russell-sized mobile phone had not yet melted. I grabbed my Filofax and the

handset and ran back up the path. Derrida had not been too bold, just unlucky. I flipped through the pages. Circumstances had changed for both of us. I'd heard he was living in Texas, apparently minding his own business for a change. It was nine a.m. in Austin, and after a few calls I found

him en route to a show of early Coach House titles in Special Collections at the University. 'Dick,' I said, 'I need a hand.' 'You up the creek again, boy?' he shouted. I glanced at Derrida. He looked old. He'd sunk to a crouch and was feeling about with his hands to support himself. I

described our predicament. Derrida listened intently, and began singing, his voice husky. '*Sous le pont Mirabeau coule la Seine ....*' On the other end Dick seemed distracted. 'See what I can do,' he said. '*Sous le pont Mirabeau ....*' 'Hey,' he said, 'you owe me, kid.' 'Hurry, Dick.' I heard a double beep. 'You still got that first of Bowering's *Baseball*?' I nodded. 'It's mine,' he bellowed, laughed, and hung up. '*Vienne la nuit, sonne l'heure ....*' I glanced at Derrida, who was grinning. 'Hold on, please,' I said. And he did for exactly eighteen minutes until over the hill another chopper

appeared, barrelling toward us. As it hovered overhead, young Israeli soldiers crowded the open door with their rifles at the ready. I gave the thumbs up. A young sergeant frowned. The pilot came around again and scrutinized us from another angle. I could see the sharpshooter inside the

door watching us carefully, unsympathetically. Derrida was tiring. The rotors were kicking up sand; it was spitting into our eyes and throats. Derrida began coughing. Without warning, he slumped. I vaulted over the fence and kneeled against him, leaning into him to keep him upright

and his foot in place. I waved to the impassive young men in the chopper. 'Hurry,' I cried. Dehydrated, buffeted by the wash, Derrida seemed to be losing consciousness. A bungee cord was released into the air above us; hand over hand they let it down, and it was soon within our reach.

I slipped the cord under his armpits, then under mine, then around our shoulders, and took a turn around the philosopher's wrist as one does when shinnying up a rope in the gymnasium. '*Tenez-vous*,' I shouted through the roar and blast of the chopper. Derrida opened his eyes and

offered up a timid, hesitant smile. At the sergeant's signal I stood and pressed down on Derrida's shoulders as hard as I could, pushing him fiercely into the dry hills of the Galilee. The helicopter began to rise. I dug my fingers into his back, forcing him into the grit, resisting the vibration and

attenuation in the cord. It was humming. I was knocked off balance and recovered quickly, fearful of crushing the human beetle beneath me, more fearful of displacing his foot. From the air we must have resembled crabs fighting, or mating. I grabbed at a rock formation, holding on for dear

life while keeping my heels planted firmly in Derrida's back. He groaned. The co-pilot looked anxious. '*Êtes-vous prêts?*' I asked. I could see the trigger below our feet. My fingers were slipping. The helicopter rose higher; the cord was hard and thin. The phone in my pocket began ringing.

Derrida glanced up. '*Ne repondes pas*,' he said. I turned my head to the sky, into the stinging dust and particles. High above us, gazing into the demon soulscape of the Gadarene swine, a young sergeant extended her arm and gave the thumbs-up once, twice, three times. I let go. I remember

hurtling into the sky, the flash of fire, the percussive roar and smoke of the explosion falling below us at breath-taking speed, then we were even with the young sergeant, shrieking, Derrida and I in mid-air, human scantling, accelerating at a rate more extreme than the helicopter itself, which was

struggling to gain altitude before gravity had its way with us, which occurred moments later. 'Hold on,' I said, as Derrida cried out. We plunged back to earth, into the swirling cloud of dust and sand only to be yanked out of it once again, inches before spattering onto a large boulder,

and whipped back up into the blue sky, and so we were flung—high and low, back and forth, gripping the narrow bungee cord—in harrowing but diminishing parabolas until the young soldiers managed to pull us aboard, first the philosopher then myself. We lay panting on the metal

deck. Derrida was exhausted and exhilarated. The phone rang. Dick. 'I'm sorry,' I said. 'No, we just got in. We're fine. Thanks.' He reminded me about the book. 'Watch your back,' he said. 'And tell that ungrateful frog we done everything the Communists done, only better, and we

didn't have to go and be Commies to do it.' I looked at Derrida, vibrating on the armoured deck with his eyes closed. Was he relishing or rueing his reprieve? 'Just remind him of who really runs the show.' He caught my hesitation. 'Listen,' he said. 'Things change. Friends change.' On either

side, curious young men and women sat with weapons on their laps. 'This isn't a joke,' he said. 'Capiche?' 'Dick?' 'I'm going to have to let your boss in on this,' he said. 'And remember what I said. Watch your back.' I heard another phone ringing. 'Don't forget my book. And don't be a

chump.' 'I won't,' I said, hearing the line go dead. The old hunter was sleeping. So much for the chapel floor at Sussita. The chopper dropped us at the car. We squeezed Derrida into the front seat and the young officer wanted to know what sort of big shots we were. 'We're just grateful,' I

The Dead of Winter

I'm still yours, it seems, on this December night, on this cold ferry deck
in this indescribable night of horizontal rain
on this sad, red shore
where I began.

What were you all doing here?

I suppose you loved me, but it's not true.
You were all too proud and parasitical
for that.
It came with the poverty, I guess,
the pilings, the splintered wood
the blighted trellis
and the resentment
at the irrelevance
of your station.
It came with the territory,
and that you got
for next to nothing.

Evergreen Playground

That island through the scupper is a broken line
of brotherly love.
A mirage.
A verb, the purse.
A hearse.

'Do you let them kiss you?'
An eagle screeches,
drops to a snag.

He flicks a scale off the gunwale with his finger.
'Why am I here?' he wonders.
'Why can I not live here without these ghosts?'
A priest watches squid hurtling around the wharf under the light.
'They are like ghosts,' he thinks.
She is squatting against the door, polishing the doorplate.
The world is filled with men in boots kicking everything.
Who cannot imagine a more efficient, less smelly tube?
This is the night they check for hoppers.
A wind is rising. He glances out at the narrows.
The girls try to get out of bed before their father, or their uncle
comes in to wake them.
Sometimes they're not gentle.
'That new Sister slapped her around real good.'

A Valentine

for Marian

Intending to kneel at your cat door like a raccoon with its
bright eyes insisting 'I'll do as I please and you'll
forgive me,' I was roused from a dream by a ring from the Seine where bits
of chocolate biscuit cheer up a room overlooking a school
and a green bookstall clamped to a wall on the Pont Marie
specializing in those movie mags in rotting plastic bags
the French specialize in—scholarly, sort of, and slightly prurient. In Paris
Freud still orients the void. And like that bridge, our love never sags.
The joints could use pointing, some panes quiver in their sockets,
but a peck on the cheek can lead to a hug, and a hug to a smooch and a
smooch to a tender word, of which too many languish in pockets,
unspoken, forgotten. 'Throw down your cell phone, your agenda—
and sing,' they proclaim, 'like the instrument you are!' You'll find
a touch may incite the flesh, but the tongue tickles the mind.

The Anvil

Spirit's history is its act. Spirit is only what it does, and its act is to make itself the object of its own consciousness, to apprehend itself as Spirit, explaining itself to itself. This self-apprehension is Spirit's very being and principle; and the fulfilment of this apprehension is at one and the same time the externalization of Spirit and the transition beyond it. To say it in formal terms, we can speak of our apprehending that apprehension anew; and then the return of Spirit into itself after its externalization is Spirit at a higher stage than the initial apprehension.

G.W.F. Hegel, Appendix to The Philosophy of Right (1821)

My foster parents or guardians didn't teach me to hate the social division in our little world. They could not, nor did they have to. It was in the air we breathed, the humble fare we ate, the poverty which was ever their lot, the search for fuels to fend off winter's cold; our need to 'crook the knee' to the gentry, to keep on the 'right side' of the Laird—if we wanted the Lord to hear our prayers.

Tom McEwen, The Forge Glows Red (1974)

Of Tom McEwen I sing: orphan, blacksmith, journalist, red. Son of Stonehaven, where Butcher Cumberland torched pews on the High Street; a father at the age of 19, who sailed with only his conscience for Montréal; whose first Canadian paycheque came at the Morden Blacksmith and

Machine Works in 1912; who sent for his wife and bairn at year's end, moving on to Winnipeg and Swift Current; whose war was never spoken of; who on returning ran the forge at the Wilson Brothers Ranch in Harris, Sask.; who looked on as his wife died of the Spanish flu; who in the

name of social justice threw his lot in with the Socialist Party of Canada and, moving the four kids to Saskatoon, the Saskatchewan Worker's Party and the CPC; whose comrades included Arthur 'Slim' Evans and a reformed Wobbly, 'T-Bone' Slim, the Borstal Boy, the Party's first sergeant-at-

arms; who, as branch Secretary, funnelled his fury into *The Furrow*, countering the syndicalist drift in the IWW and the OBU; who remarried; who as Party organizer for District 7 from 1927–29 often took along Frank Gledhill, a Yorkshireman from Kuroli, Sask., to ask, 'Why is a farmer like a dill pickle? Because when you squeeze him he will squirt, but not always in the right direction!' (I can hear their voices, '*Arise ye workers from your slumbers* ...,' the gallant anthem of the end, not the means); who was a founding member of the National and Executive Committees of the Worker's

Unity League, the Party's legal arm; who was in 1930 beaten by Toronto police for 'obstructing traffic' and handed 15 days in the Don Jail; who led the Canadian delegation to the 5th World Congress of the Red International of Labour Unions in Moscow in 1931; who was locked away in

Kingston for two years for the Work or Wages Campaign ('membership in an illegal organization' under Section 98); who held the line, without deviation; who regarded mass graves and summary executions as the lesser evil in a just civil war; whose faith remained unshaken by the betrayal of

the Menshevist splitters of the Trotskyist-Zinovievist bloc; who welcomed the 281,000 tractor Spring of 1934; who internalized Comrade Stalin's May 1935 proclamation to the Red Army Academies that 'technique decides everything' would henceforth be replaced by 'cadres decide

everything'; who fused his will to the soul of the Soviet people during the extermination of the Bukharin-Trotsky fiends; who in Aleksei Stakhanov's heroic 102 tons of coal in a single, sacrificial shift divined a new tide of Socialist emulation; who rallied the disheartened in the

Relief Camp Workers Union and the On to Ottawa Trek; who regarded Stalin's 98.6 per cent of the 1937 vote as a steel fist to the throat of international Fascism; who a year later accepted a job in the Comintern—the Comrade Leader's 'meat-grinder'—moving to Russia, a blacksmith, to

take up his duties on the Anglo-American desk; and so, mid-chapter, the hammer falls silent for two years while Beria's men carved the eyes out of Zinaida Raikh and pounded on the doors of Isaac Babel, Mandelstam and two million more; whose Comintern boss, André Marty—one of the hard men who'd stoked the Revolution's charnel house—had entered History in 1919 when red flags cracked in the Black Sea wind aboard the *Waldeck-Rousseau* and French sailors roared '*Debout les damnés de la terre, Debout les forçats de la faim*,' who as Chief Political Commissar

for the International Brigades built a concentration camp for his own men, who for his vicious reprisals was dubbed the 'butcher of Albacete' (McEwen's two boys in the Mac-Paps steered clear, Hemingway hatched a loathsome portrait in *For Whom the Bell Tolls*), who siphoned gold bars

from Spain's central bank into China where McEwen's daughter, a nurse, had joined Norman Bethune's transfusion unit in Yan'an, Bethune having airmailed from Hong Kong, 'I refuse to condone, by passivity, or default, the wars which greedy men make against others.' Canadians,

bent on justice, banking on butchers. In headier days, for example, Herbert Norman, in 1930s Cambridge, recruiting Indian undergrads to the Party, admitting to V.G. Kiernan, his junior, that one must have a mechanism—in his case the movies—with which to keep depression from the

door. Tom, did lilacs bloom at your Moscow door? To what did you sign your name? Samuel Darcy, attending the Seventh Party Congress in July 1935, took note of those missing: 'Looking for friends I had made on previous trips I found many had perished in struggle or even by being

passive,' he wrote. There's no mention, Tom, of Eisenstein's *Die Walküre* at the Bolshoi, or of Jews vanishing from your hallways, or of the convolutions of the faithful when it appeared they'd been pimping for Hitler. If wickedness is an aphid, is idealism its ant? Who, in 1940, was

incarcerated at Headingley, in Manitoba, and later, for the duration of the war, at the internment camp in Hull; who ran for parliament as a labour organizer in 1945—in the Yukon; who in 1950 was mailing cancelled stamps to his friend Lily in Toronto to raise money for the *Pacific Tribune*, which, for twenty-five years, he published in Vancouver; whose granddaughter I adored all one summer and the next, and the next; whom I'll cherish always for his account of how, at a Mine Worker's Union convention in Calgary in the late 1930s, the delegates, returning to their hotel,

were startled to recognize one of the guests parked in a wheelchair in the lobby, and how, when they refused to go to their rooms unless he was removed, the proprietor, learning the man's name, wheeled him out onto the sidewalk, leaving Dan Campbell, Ginger Goodwin's assassin in the

bush near Cumberland in 1918, to fend for himself; whose book's title recalls Georgi Dimitrov, the Bulgarian communist who quoted Goethe at the 1933 Reichstag trial: *'Amboss oder Hammer sein'*—'You've got to be the anvil or the hammer'—a benison for butchers Cumberland, Marty,

Mao, Stalin and Dimitrov himself, and would you prefer to 'pound or be pounded upon?' I know who dies in bed. Who, on receiving one of 5,000 Lenin Centenary medals reserved for foreign apparatchiks in 1970, praised the 'imperishable science of Marxist-Leninism;' who gently

departed this aphid world on Irving Berlin's 100th birthday at the age of 97; whose perishable, well-loved soul renounced any wayward inclinations by sacrificing itself to History, becoming one, in the dark night of the century, with the hard men of progress. McEwen's was the Cosmic

Anvil; its augury a messianic Reckoning. You must come clean, he'd tell the fathers in the mines, the kids in the woods, their women, the limping veterans of Flanders who watched over him in the cells: *Which side are you on?* Did he waver? It was not a wavering business. Hegel courted excess:

'World history is a court of judgement—because in its implicit and explicit *universality*, the *particular* is present only as *ideal*.' Last week I swam in Walden Pond. Today, north of Ladysmith, the last t'ai chi sign has crashed from its pole. Old tracts rot in thrift store crates. One night I turned on my father and demanded to know why he'd not signed up for the International Brigades. Imagine walking in the door to a show trial chaired by your pus-faced son, the commissar. What was I after, humiliating the fragile man who loved me? Then again, does World History give a fig for a

few squished aphids? I raged against the love I longed for; I lunged in sorry ignorance at every decoy. But my family has prospered thanks to the genocides. Property values are up. The shovel, *au fond*, is the law. Tom, you inhabited the Ideal to perpetuate the Ideal. In how many ways have I

failed the hands, eyes and hearts that have reached out for me? Our running lights bloody the water. What is more hopeful than the little word that tries to be the world? Hopeful? No wonder the *ideal* is like diseased flesh to a bluebottle. Tom McEwen, how did you console yourself?

To lyric's to say: I've seen
in overflow
I join my dog on earth

Fairview

for George Bowering

This crustal pile underwent Jurassic to Eocene east-directed crustal thickening coeval with the obduction and accretion of allochthonous terranes to the ancestral margin of the North American craton.

Robert Nicholas Spark

I'm riding, George
above the boars

on a flank of the fiery town
of Oliver hard by that herd of

Stelkia stallions on a hillside
just below the Rattler

in Fairview
where hands clapped

once, where everything
happened

but they didn't call it that,
or anything,

they thought about it
but

they were in it;
if they were

puzzled by it
we don't know.

The sea was here
but they weren't,

they were Americans
or wishing they were

as we did, and trying
to look down someone's

shirt and I can't say
who God was to them

but he was and is
this not a perfect

day for wedding
snaps and swimming

which, let's face it,
doesn't attract flies the

way horses do, even if
this mare is invisible

the livery's invisible
the dry goods are

the whole town's
invisible

and whatever happened
to dry goods and was

there a wet goods store here
do you know?

At my wedding
I'll keep off the sand

you won't catch me in those
elastic-topped trousers or

riding the mechanical bull.
Why is the world such an

inscrutable muon?
What did we expect?

If I say God
is God present?

Why am I so afraid of him?
What did God ever do to me?

Let's pass National Treasure
legislation and nominate God

as an inductee. Why not
spell his name the Canadian

way? *Goud.*
Listen!

Sage warblers.
I'm riding through the valley

of the shadow of
the Monashee Gneiss

in a town that left behind
its lilacs in 1909.

Ivie Anderson
was only four then

and I'm still fearful.
Let's change that word

to Fairview.
Before you can say

craton
it'll evaporate

and be forgotten
like this townsite,

a meadow now
where my little cayuse

is munching a lock
of yellow grass.

Old guys may
remember,

whatever
that means,

but when we go
lilacs will still bloom

it will be cold
in the shadow

and hot as a snake's
neck in July.

Up the valley
the dismantled planks

of the largest city
north of San Francisco

will rattle on their rafters
when it blows.

Old guys will know why
they don't fit.

A Square Sonnet

A square is what I long to see on miles
and miles of dark road. Mirrored window, eye
to eye or eyed from patches of dark blue glass,
the light pulls (yanks) me forward. Silk is a liquid
mirror suspended from ice. Don't you yearn for
pain to rouze your senses?
The song she took the high road on is not
a cricket's song; my lover's lips are sweeter
and sadder. What *if* the world is tuned to plum
or quince? A heaven on earth, and sweet at night
beneath the moon? I fall upon the grasses,
old songs abide, I'm possessed. Roots
redden in me. I approach,
trailing lilac, and fall to my knees.
I thee kiss, my earth, my beloved.

North Atlantic Drift

in a crib in Inverness

in a cart in Ullapool

in a garden in Am Ploc Ard

in a teller's cage in Kamloops

in a log house near Knutsford

in a boat on Lac le Jeune

in tying a fly

in a shuddering sigh

in a stranger's cry

can we have peace without justice?

on a mustang in Falkland

in a democrat at Dog Lake

in the cellar at Strathyre

in a letter from her mother

in tears when he told her

in a Vancouver armoury

in the kilt of his fathers

on a milk train to Montréal

on duckboards in France

on a ward in Matlock Bath

in a nerve in his leg

in a rage on returning

in his daughter's sobbing

can there be peace without justice?

in a boathouse in Brentwood

in the sea at Yellow Point

on a coach in Parksville

in a red-baiting crowd

in a burning garage

in a fiery house

in the bar in Nanaimo

in the Qualicum Men's

in the bags you kept packing

grandfather, come near

can there be peace without justice?

in debt and deeper

on the overnight sleeper

in a carbonized castle

in a scuttle of coal

in a bucket of turnips

in a shed in the garden

in shame and in silence

in a heart divided

can there be peace without justice?

Love, Again

Who has not fallen
out of love
with asking why?

More and more are just leaving
their pyjama pants on
in the morning.

Nothing exudes
the familiar more than
the unfamiliar.

My elderly relative
who opts for sex
with strangers,

for instance. How can you
call them strangers?
Is it sex?

The morning is cool.
August light
below.

At a glance there is no sex
taking place
on this plane

although more and more
are just leaning back
against their seats

in the upright position
and closing
their eyes.

The Other Side

I awoke this morning
on the other side.

I felt calm, and loved
and nothing worked.

Everything had a new name.
I tried so hard to keep it that way.

The angels begged and begged,
and flew weakly against the screen.

Le Rouge Gorge

Prunes with lamb tagine.
Heaven.
A glass of the Corsican.
Sublime.
A little talk of casting a fly.
Bells ringing.

~~Rue Grenier sur l'eau~~ *Allée des Justes*

I dropped this as yet
unwritten poem
on the sidewalk
outside a school
the Nazis pulled up to
in trucks
for the purpose of
transporting Jewish children
to Auschwitz.
This narrow street.
This friendly sidewalk.
Perhaps this very day
just a little more than
sixty years ago.

At an ancient bridge we take the
rutted road up through
the trees
in
Poitou. A cock pheasant in
silhouette. The dog's
nose lifts. Oaks,
hawthorns and
a swallow in
flat light, sun
hot, wheat
falls away
into the river. We arrive at the crest. I'm told, 'This is where two resistants were murdered.'
In Port-Louis, strolling late at night with the family, having skirted the Mini-Golf, the
seventeenth-century Spanish fortifications, the nineteenth and twentieth-century French garrison, the
neon green of a disco leaking under a door, I crack a joke about Nazis. 'Don't, please,'
I'm told. 'Up
there in the
dark you'll find
resistants' graves.
On the way back
we stop to admire
a house with white
gables in the lamp
light. 'Here the
Vichy gendarmerie
set up its
HQ.'

'All I'm Allowed'

The little players have shuttered their egg, or is that a turret?
The boy's too bald to be a turnip, or is that a boil?
(Or) is that a lobster boat scotching about in the seals?
Their bodies are (now) with me every day,
whose forebears were nursed by leopards.

Lions

She no longer
pretends the world
is dead.

It was a long haul.

Cocktail parties, parades, humiliations, bewilderment,
all of us keeping
our mouths shut
for years.
Exhausting.

'Oh, aren't you good little girls,'
she purrs to the dandelions,
reaching out from
her chair,
'you *are* good little girls!
Isn't this the best place
in the world?'

She laughs.

'How do they know what they're doing?
They're doing what they're doing!'

Photograph courtesy of the Imperial War Museum, London, Q 92160.

Over Olean, or The Misuse of Reticence

for Colin and Graham Ritchie

> *How could the artist, the soldier in the artist, not praise God for the collapse of a peaceful world with which he was fed up, so exceedingly fed up?*
>
> Thomas Mann (1914)

> *All the subject provinces of the Empire to me were not worth one dead English boy.*
>
> T.E. Lawrence, *Seven Pillars of Wisdom* (Oxford Ed., 1922)

> *In the silence something happens. A well-remembered voice says: 'Father.'*
>
> J.M. Barrie, *A Well-Remembered Voice* (1918)

As it was related to me by my great aunt Marjorie Acland on Salt Spring Island thirty-four years ago, smoking hand-rolled cigarettes with a wry smile and a glass of orange, grapefruit and raisin wine steeped for three weeks in a Medalta crock in the kitchen. There'd be baked potato, half a

cucumber and ham on the plate with a plum-coloured clay pot of Coleman's. My fingers smelled of alder, lemon balm and salt from rubbing off slug. I was twenty-six. It's dawn. Hercules are landing in Kabul. She'd have been twenty-six in the winter of 1916-1917, with two little ones,

sharing a flat in London while Bevil was in France. The flap over fruitcake or socks had fizzled; spy scandals, Jewish plots and rumours of mutiny distracted. Trains left daily with pink-cheeked boys. My Chevaliers of the Twitching Pestle, Wyndham Lewis, Ezra Pound, T.S. Eliot, were

preoccupied with sex: getting it, imagining it, parading it in a sneer of innuendo and homophobic yawping (poor Tom!). Bertrand Russell in his *Autobiography* recalls steamy encounters that winter with twenty-year-old actress and anti-conscription activist Collette O'Niel. 'The first time that I

was ever in bed with her,' he wrote years later—neglecting to add he'd just sprung from Vivienne Eliot's arms—'(we did not go to bed the first time we were lovers, as there was too much to say), we heard suddenly a shout of bestial triumph in the street. I leapt out of bed and saw a Zeppelin falling in flames. The thought of brave men dying in agony was what caused the triumph in the street.' Below, in the cold dusk, Chicago stockyards glimmer where thousands of startled horses were corralled, branded, broken and driven daily into railway cars bound for the 'purifying fire.'

Elgar, to a friend, four weeks in, '…oh! my beloved animals—the men—and women can go to hell—but my horses;—I walk round & round this room cursing God for allowing dumb brutes to be tortured—let Him kill his human beings but—how CAN HE? Oh, my horses.' In December

1916, David Milne fled New York for Bishop's Pond. Two years later, one of the King's Guests, he was at Vimy, painting. I celebrate *Aerodrome*, *Chamblain-L'Abbé* and *Wrecked Tanks near Sanctuary Wood* as works of transcendent imagination. We're flying into the infant night above 'Alleghany

Indian Reservation' on Cathay Pacific Flight 888. A baby is wailing. We're over Olean on the serrated edge of a thunderstorm. Lightning. America seems to manifest a mystical receptivity to storms. Tomorrow we'll congratulate ourselves on the felicity of 'levels of blessedness.' Marjorie's

flatmate, Enid Ritchie—her sister's schoolmate—had a new baby named Dick, and every day, in drizzle or in sleet, they'd circumnavigate the Serpentine with prams. 'Finish the ham.' Aunt Marjorie pushes the plate my way. London in the winter of 1916 was a dark estuary, a tide of

black satin, black stockings, black skirts, black hats, black Oxfords, black veils. Widows, on a wet, black bough. A press photo of a Fleet Street wall shows a large hand-written placard: **IF YOU ARE A WHITEMAN PROVE YOUR COLOUR AND COURAGE NOW.** An intimate Whitehall

gathering urged poets early on to undermine U.S. neutrality. Hardy obliged with 'Men who March Away.' C.P. Sanger to Russell a year later: 'Masefield writing up the Dardanelles—has been allowed to see some official documents and so on. It is most disheartening that literary men of standing should try to make a mere calamity "epic" for American consumption.' (Hardy to Galsworthy, three years later, 'I cannot do patriotic poems very well ....') Enid's mother had been urging her to attend meetings at the Royal Albert Hall. 'Why would I?' asked Enid, 'I'm not you.'

Christmas came, with talk of peace, New Year's went, bells rang, they had snow, then teeth, then colds. Marge's Bevil lurched around the flat on leave for a week, half-catatonic. Winter in the nursery. Boiling eggs, nursing babies, folding nappies, blowing noses, pleasing parents. Beef was

scarce. Squirrels could be bought, or a spotted woodpecker. Crossing the Queensborough Bridge into Manhattan the cabbie brags about his sons. One's in the Gulf. 'Called home yesterday,' he said. 'Couldn't say where from, his ship, you know ....' It's 2005, September 22nd, and oil fires

blaze in Amara—paradise of the stuttering, limping vessels of God. 'Potato? It won't keep.' Despite absurd lengths by critics to be coy, there is no victor in the final notes of Lincoln Centre's *Capriccio*, or Strauss's. The ancient duel's revived whenever mischief rules the heart, whenever one

becomes two; to lose one's head is a caprice. Ibn 'Arabi, after Al-Junayd: 'The colour of the water is the colour of its receptacle.' I'm a civil servant subsidized by oil profits extracted at gunpoint to assert division, to enchant initiates with abstractions and transcendentalist hand-wringing; pricey

pouches of *bufala* notwithstanding, there *is* here. Enid's mother kept on at her. 'You'll feel better,' she chirped. Enid saw no truth in that, nor respite in truth. Eggs, milk, babies, nappies, these were her haven. Red-eyed women, sobbing in the street, confused her, she felt shameful. A girl next

door was turning yellow. In 1760, Sir Robert Davers, a young baronet from Suffolk, entered the hickory forests of New York to live among the Hurons in a bid to liberate himself from hereditary depression. After two years he was hacked to pieces by Chippewas. We pass the Morning Star

Café on 9th at 57th thronged with midnight noshers. Thomas Hart Benton stormed home to Missouri after appearing on *Time*'s Christmas Eve cover in 1934. 'Communism is a joke everywhere in the United States except New York,' he announced. Her mother did not relent.

'Have you read James Hewatt McKenzie? I've still got one of his books. She took us all for tea at the Ritz, in the Palm Court. I don't know what she was thinking, with five of us jumping up and down every second. *If a Soldier Die*. It's in the bookcase.' Enid's pale face. 'Pull yourself together,'

said her mother, 'you can't go on like this.' And Enid asking, 'Why?' And then, 'Why not?' Young girls polished the foliage. Dick threw up a little cream. 'I'm not superstitious,' said Enid. She was thinking of the Goose Lake Road. 'Margie will take the children, won't you?' A week later she

caved in. 'What does one do with boys?' Wash often. It is about folds and lips, thought Enid. I walked out of the Holiday Inn into Atlantic light. Novels on a table to finance guerrilla theatre. Quinces in our Vancouver garden, yellow first, then brown and mottled. On Marge's lawn that

fall, crop after crop of Shaggy Manes. They arrived early. Enid's mother laid her fox across the seats. Women rushed into powder rooms. Twitching and talking, then a small, thick woman, in the footlights. Six thousand widows sat to attention. Invoking a god unknown to Enid—with a

cruel beak, perhaps—the woman bowed her head. She appeared to have no shadow. The widows bent their heads. Intoning, she began to rock, and her fierce, jay eyes scanned their faces. Enid was dismayed. The woman was sweating, lifting her chin, her eyeballs rolling back into ivory

sockets, hair falling on her face, and it seemed she might fall backward. A star shell exploded, the room streamed with light. Enid was lofted up and away from her body, airborne without fear or hesitation, high above the Albert Hall. She was crying, and giving birth. She reached out for her

the first-born. Far from her mother's anxieties, Enid had been corresponding with a young man punching cows in Burn's Lake who'd promised to visit on his way home. About the same time, T.E. Lawrence received a pair of Colt automatics from an American lady. 'I have a horrible fear

that the Turks do not intend to go to war,' he wrote her, 'for it would be an improvement to have them reduced to Asia Minor ....' With snow in the high country, the cowpuncher, Dick Ritchie, mailed a letter and followed the Thompson south, carrying his chaps. Marjorie lights a cigarette.

'Does anyone know,' she asks, 'why everything turned out so dreadfully?' Follow the big hill out of town, turn right at Knutsford onto the Fish Lake Road, and a mile or two along you'll find a gate. Take the road through the pines, up the rise past Brook's shack, down around the corner, bump,

bump, there's a track through the tall grass, you'll see a row of cottonwoods on the hill and in a little draw, a log house with green burlap on the walls and the chair in the corner where I sat in his lap and it was the end of October, the aspen were yellow and quaking, stars filled the sky and

he asked me to marry him as the cruisers *Goeben* and *Breslau* steamed into Sevastopol and Odessa to destroy the Russian Black Sea fleet. Turkey was *in the game.* The woman moved her lips. Feet shuffled, heads bent, six thousand faces lifted into light. 'I've a message for Enid. Is there an Enid

in the hall?' Hurrying back to England, Dick Ritchie reported to his regiment, the Norfolks, 2nd Battalion. Enid followed, trailing a chaperone. War smiles on the second chancers. Syrians in Canada appealed to Prime Minister Borden, offering up to 50,000 volunteers from North and

South America in return for the promise of self-government in their homeland. Politely declined. Britain had no intention of sharing the spoils. There's likely not a soul alive today who'll recall a summer morning in 1915 and a steamer lined with grinning lads in khaki, among their number

Lt. R.D. Ritchie—married six weeks—chuting down an English river to the sea. Destination: Mespot, or Mesopotamia, Greek, according to a textbook, for the land 'between the rivers.' For Europeans, the ones to embrace it, the name's virtue lay in geographical imprecision, which is to

say that it afforded unrivalled opportunities for Great Power bullying and treachery. In the previous century, for obscure reasons, a well-bred lady, flushed with pleasure, might have cried out, 'How perfectly *Mesopotámian!*' A word swells to consume the world. Tom Eliot, twenty-seven

in 1916—as was T.E. Lawrence—and bingeing on Nietzsche, was under strict orders to report to his mother in St. Louis after rendezvous with the great and good in London. In one letter the war intruded. He'd been to Waterloo Station to see Vivienne's brother off. 'I heard both officers and

men, at the station, returning,' he wrote, 'the men mostly drunk, and their women crying; the officers and their women very quiet.' As if a young duke had glanced out the window of a passing landau. How embarrassingly un-*Mesopotámian* to stumble on such dismaying displays of affection.

All the 'men', by this time, were conscripts. 'There are no conscientious objectors among the Vortex,' Eliot later wrote to Conrad Aiken, 'they are all in another set, mostly localised in Bloomsbury.' Officers, no doubt. Nations must win wars. To outrun the German fleet, Britain's

new Dreadnoughts had been converted from coal to oil. To guarantee its fuel supply, the Admiralty had taken an interest in a 60-year concession developed by an Englishman, William Knox D'Arcy, for five-sixths of the Persian empire. In 1909, Donald Smith, Lord Strathcona, was

encouraged to invest £50,000. The Anglo-Persian Oil Company was quickly incorporated with Strathcona as chairman and a garrison of British-Indian cavalry at the wellhead. The Crown acquired a two-thirds share of Anglo-Persian in 1912, including wells, the pipeline, a refinery in

Abadan and mineral concessions, and signed a secret twenty-year deal with the Royal Navy. When the Turkish Petroleum Company was incorporated in London soon after, APOC acquired a half interest. In June 1914, the Grand Vizier of the Sublime Porte offered the promise of a

petroleum lease to TPC in the vilayets of Mosul and Baghdad. Within a year Britain and France would meet in secret to dismember the Vizier's empire. France claimed Syria, Lebanon and northern Mesopotamia; Britain—Palestine, Trans-Jordan, central and southern Mesopotamia

including the Anglo-Persian oilfields. The criminally incompetent Lord Hardinge, viceroy of India, had been urging the outright annexation of Basra Vilayet as 'a second Egypt.' With war declared, he dispatched a division of Indian troops from Bombay. Not long after Dick Ritchie

set sail for England, Indian Expeditionary Force 'D', with His Majesty's Ships *Odin*, *Espiegle* and *Dalhousie*, laid siege to the towns of the Shatt al-Arab. Fighting was bloody. On November 23rd, 1914, in smoldering Basra, beneath a Union Jack, Chief Political Officer Percy Cox, who'd

brokered a deal with the Sheikh of Mohammerah for the island of Abadan, took the salute: '… we have no enmity or ill-will against the population,' said he in Arabic, 'to whom we hope to prove good friends and protectors.' The putrescent limbs of beautiful young men were shoveled into

ditches. Cox's men set to work bribing tribal chieftains. Indian 'coolies' arrived to build roads, dikes, bridges, railways, barracks and wharves. Water and food spoiled overnight. Cholera struck like a bayonet, gutting the invaders slipping in the toffee-coloured slime. Four hundred and fifty

'volunteers' were shipped from Indian jails to shovel out the garrison latrines. Poverty, misery and a crippling rate of incarceration were British India's secret weapons. In return for a pardon, or its promise, 16,000 Indian prisoners signed on for the Jail Labour Corps, earning half the daily

loyalty would lie with those sympathetic to their aspirations. Overture discouraged. Glory-hungry, reckless with ill-health and heatstroke, Nixon urged recklessness on London; in August, with Hardinge's blessing, he prevailed. Major General Charles Vere Ferrers Townshend, scion of the

Townshend whose cartoons had humiliated Wolfe at Québec—a man called a semi-lunatic by General Haig—was ordered north with two divisions and the promise of reinforcements. 'This is what they call in New York running the show at "scalp rates",' he protested, but he could not

resist a shot at glory. 'Baghdad by Christmas!' was the cry. October 1915. Charles Chaplin is screening rushes for *Easy Street*. He's twenty-six. A steamer churns through the chocolate ooze above the bar into the Shatt al-Arab. A small tender slithers into a disintegrating bank, Lt. Dick

Ritchie steps ashore into the plague-ridden shit hole known as Mespot. Shoals menace the yellow river, bugs swarm, skin blisters and shrivels in the sun. In the occupied city of Sinbad, Dick is feverish, disoriented. Everything he touches smells of sweet, dried shit. God is thick here, and

careless, on this river of Paradise with its cargo of corpses where, ninety years on, detainees are forced to swim or drown at the muzzle of a British gun. Heartsick, trembling, Dick marches his troops north to join the 18th Brigade at Aziziyah. The men of the 7th Rajhputs, the 110th Mahratta

Light Infantry and the 120th Rajputana Infantry are sullen, their ranks haunted, in the words of Moukbil Bey, by '*le moral douteux*.' What can Dick tell these sons and fathers? They'll soon rejoin their families in India? Bowel management absorbs his waking hours. He fails to remember his

bed at home, or his dog. He struggles to keep his uniform clean. Men with dark eyes follow each move. The mess frightens him. Amara, *the garden of tears*. Dick might have gleaned a little Shuswap in Burns Lake, but he's incapable of conversing with the men who dug the hole and threw into it the decomposing body of the officer he's replacing. He thinks of wooden cattle chutes. The Sikhs and Hindus seem to be indifferent, but the Muslim sepoys, who revere the Turkish sultan as their Caliph, have no heart for killing their brothers on this holy ground. Some vanish into the desert,

into the Prophet's footsteps (peace and blessings of Allah be with them). Some hack fingers off, preferring paws to the accusation of Crusader. The colonized body consumes itself. 'The rivers flow with liquid mud,' wrote Robert Byron in the 1930s. 'The air is composed of mud refined into

a gas.' Expeditionary Force 'D' straggled north. Temperatures plunged. Mud froze. The *sharqi* is a blizzard of stone. 'There are flies that bite like bulldogs everywhere,' noted Aubrey Herbert. What did Enid know? The snapshot in her album shows Dick leaning on a ship's rail in an open-necked

tropical khaki shirt. His mouth gapes, his eyes squint past the lens as if to avoid our stare, to distract us from what he has witnessed. It's a portrait of a man's presentiments: of choking, submersion, decay. War's hardships got Alexander Graham Bell cogitating. Suppose the brain's

electro-magnetic waves could be harnessed as a telepathic medium, linking trench to parlour, sick bay to nuptial bed. 'Men can do nearly everything else by electricity already,' he wrote, 'and I can imagine them with coils of wire about their heads coming together for communication of thought

by induction.' It was in the air. 'I had many ideas for feature pictures,' Chaplin wrote of that time. 'One was a trip to the moon, a comic spectacle showing the Olympic Games there … I thought of … a radioelectric hat that could register one's thoughts, and the trouble I get into when I put it

on my head and am introduced to the moon man's sexy wife.' In the Morningstar Café, I was thinking of José Limón and about how the altruist's struggle for independence is the hard man's civil war, when in walked a roly-poly man, a faun in rags who hopped onto a stool and looked up like a lonely baby. Eggs were poached, coffee poured, but not for him. The Mom behind the counter said it was time to move along. He reached for the plastic lid on the chocolate cake and lifted it into the air. 'Be nice,' she said, 'you know the rule.' He stared and sat back. She gave him

a look. He replaced the cover and leaned forward. 'Just be nice,' she said. He made a face and raged out, banging the door. Menaced by sand flies, lice, mosquitoes, rancid meat, snipers, trachoma, boils, fevers and the runs—you had to watch your step—Dick Ritchie urged his men

up the Tigris to the outskirts of Eden, sleeping under the frozen stars with a pistol beneath his head. 'This 'ere is the land of sweet F-all with a river up it,' a Canadian trooper's said to have said, in a memorable reprise of Genesis. At dusk the wind fell, the Turks crept near, calling out like

birds to their brothers. In that abattoir everyone watched his neck. On a naval base in Brittany Roland Barthes was taking his first breath. D.H. Lawrence was contesting a judicial ban on *The Rainbow*. 'I set my rainbow in the sky too soon,' he'd write, 'before, instead of after, the deluge.'

E.M. Forster was for kicking up a fuss: '... the right to literary expression is as great in war as it was ever in peace, and in far greater danger,' he wrote to Newbolt. The management of feed was critical; within weeks, they'd be gulping down light draught horse kedgeree. In *Horse Management*

on Active Service (1918), E.D. Miller laid out the diet. 'Horses want food very early in the morning and as late as possible at night ... so put in the nosebags last thing at night, 2 and 1/2 lbs. of chaff, and make the line sentries put the nose bags on first thing in the morning, say 6 a.m., and let them

have a nibble of chaff. At 7 a.m. water. They will not drink much, but some of them want it; feed with 4 lbs. of oats mixed with a handful of chaff. At 11.30 a.m. water. At 12 (noon) feed with the same. At 4.30 p.m. water. At 7 p.m. give them the remainder of the hay in nets or in the racks.'

For the purposes of triangulation, Captain Henry Aloysius Petre of the Royal Australian Flying Corps had rigged up a device resembling an abbreviated garden rake, the shaft of which he pressed to his forehead while flying. The pegs at the far end determined, by degree, the distance

of the target from a site fixed by a central prong. Motoring through hot, thin air at 50 m.p.h., or blown backwards in a gust of wind, he'd mapped out the lineaments of the ancient world. A Flying Corps Martinsyde had also spotted 18,000 Turks digging in on both banks of the Tigris at

Selman Pak—Scheherazade's Isbanir, or Ctesiphon, soon to be christened 'Pissed-upon'. And overhead, the soaring arch of Taq-e Kasra, the vault of a fortress that had shaken when the Prophet left the womb. From this shore Sassanian princes sallied forth to slice up their foes. On a

clear day you can gaze across the lake of blood to Baghdad's minarets. By now, Enid knew. Had she sent him a telegram? And Dick? He was bearing down on the sacred tomb of Selman the Persian, the saint revered as the Flag of Flags, the Prophet's barber, the terrestrial manifestation

of the Archangel Gabriel. A Zoroastrian, a Christian and a Muslim, in that order, it's said that in the whirlwind of each faith Selman encountered the ineffable voice of God. Heralded as one of the Gates of Paradise, in 627 he invented trench warfare. Ibn 'Arabi placed this song between his lips:

> *My heart can assume any shape—*
> *a pasture for gazelles, a monastery for holy men,*
> *a temple for idolaters, the pilgrims' Ka'ba,*
> *the Torah's luminous scrolls, the Book of Qur'an.*
> *I'm intoxicated by love in every guise.*
> *In whatever direction it may gallop*
> *love is my religion and my faith.*

At dawn on November 22nd 1915, the only year in which Vancouver won the Stanley Cup, with Turkish cooking fires to the north, Dick Ritchie lay shivering in a ditch. Gertrude Bell, on a secret mission to Basra, ran that same day into one of his colleagues. 'The ship is crowded,' she wrote to

her father. '… I have scraped acquaintance with a young man who came back wounded from the Persian Gulf last year and is not going back to rejoin his regiment either there or in India. He told me all about the beginning of that campaign, to my deep interest. Unfortunately he was wounded

after 11 days of it, so he could not tell me much. Helen Brassey has with her a Freeman Thomas boy who is going out to his father's staff in Bombay, and a Miss Brand. They are nice little cheerful people. We all sit at the Captain's table together.' Fresh troops had been swelling the

Ottoman trenches. Franz Boas in New York was opining on eugenics: 'The fundamental motive that prompts us to advocate eugenic measures,' he wrote, 'is perhaps not so much the idea of increasing human efficiency as rather to eliminate human suffering. The humanitarian idea of the

elimination of suffering … seems, however, opposed to the conditions under which species survive. What is an inconvenience today will be suffering tomorrow; and the effect of an exaggerated humanitarianism may be to make mankind so sensitive to suffering that the very roots of its

existence will be endangered.' Concealing the proximity of Selman's tomb from his Muslim troops, Townshend had moved the divisions up overnight. Dawn found them dazed and disoriented, diarrhoea tearing out their guts as it had Septimius Severus' legions, grubbing in the

same muck in 197. A Maurice Farman Shorthorn roared into the sky and was shot down by rifles. Its maps were hurried to Noureddine Bey. Townshend, who'd told a subaltern the night before, 'I may be very ugly, but I'm a great man,' ordered the attack. His gunboats opened fire. Their shells

them south through the tamarind groves. At Lejj, after 49 km., the survivors were heaped onto open steel barges hooked to unpredictable vessels with names like *Blosse Lynch, Mosul, Medjidieh*. Dick's battalion held the flank as the rump of Townshend's army, with horses, camels, mules and

motor vans, began its descent of the pestilential river. Raiding parties swept in, beheading terrified stragglers. Corpses bobbed on the current. Gunboats *Firefly, Comet* and *Shaitan* ran aground and were stripped, burned and scuttled. After seven days, with sleet glazing the muddy banks, a horde

of ghosts straggled into Kut and a five-month siege marked by starvation, amputation and disease. Deserters were shot, livestock slain. Muslim sepoys, undone by cassoulets of horsemeat and mule, crawled to the front line and presented themselves to Turkish marksmen for release. In January,

Australia quit the Dardanelles. Captain Petre fled to Cairo. Apollinaire, in March, took a star of shrapnel in the skull while reading Syrian history in a trench planked with corpses. In April, the pomegranates bloomed, and Capt. T.E. Lawrence sailed into Basra on the Canadian ship *Royal*

George, or *'Rolling George'*. He called on Gertrude Bell. 'We have had great talks,' she wrote her mother, 'and made vast schemes for the government of the universe. He goes up river tomorrow, where the battle is raging these days … One's extraordinarily lonely with no one of one's own.

That's why even Mr. Lawrence was such a godsend.' Setting off with 'biscuits, ten loaves, ten tins of jam and ten tins of beef,' Lawrence soon appeared in Kut with Colonel W.H. Beach and M.P. Aubrey Herbert, 'TO IF POSSIBLE PURCHASE ONE OF THE TURKISH LEADERS OF THE

MESOPOTAMIAN ARMY SUCH AS KHALIL OR NEGIB SO AS TO FACILITATE RELIEF TOWN-SHEND.' Raising a white flag, Lawrence, Beach and Herbert walked out into no-man's land where, wrote Herbert, 'we waited, with all the battlefield smells around us. It was all a plain with the river to the north and the place crawling with huge black beetles and singing flies that have been feeding on the dead.' They were left to roast, then blindfolded and taken on horses to Khalil Pasha, the Ottoman commander, who'd once encountered Herbert at an embassy dance. He was

enraged to hear that Townshend had spiked his guns. Negotiations ensued, Turkish ladies for English ladies, and a ransom of £1,000,000 was offered for the garrison at Kut. Injured prisoners were exchanged—500 Indians and Englishmen for 500 Ottomans—but even at £2,000,000 the

commander refused the dishonour of a bribe. Lawrence recorded an excellent meal 'in the Turkish style'. Two days later Townshend handed Khalil Pasha his sword. His emaciated troops were herded north; over 4,000 perished en route and in labour camps. Local Arabs were executed

as collaborators. Back in Basra, Lawrence spent several days savaging 'the Mespot gang.' George Bernard Shaw in London was experiencing CO letter-writing fatigue. One of Yeats' cousins had asked him to intervene in the case of her son. 'He seems to be, like many literary people,' he wrote

to Russell, 'helpless in practical affairs and the army is in some ways the very place for him; for he will be trained to face the inevitable, and yet have no responsibilities. He will be fed and clothed and exercised and told what to do; and he will have unlimited opportunities for thinking about

other things … I do not blame any intelligent man for trying to dodge the atrocious boredom of soldiering, if it can be dodged, but Chapelow seems to have been too helpless to make any attempt to dodge it: he simply stood gaping in the path of the steamroller.' In his chivalrous

campaign history, Moukbil Bey declared the siege of Kut 'l'un des episodes les plus glorieux de notre histoire militaire.' It took a year to expose the criminal incompetence of the British campaign. The Report of the Mesopotamia Commission (1917), Part X., Section D., 'The Misuse of Reticence', records the fate of the 3,500 sick and wounded laid out in the air for two weeks as the barges of human sludge made their way south. Major Carter, the Medical Officer in charge of the hospital ship *Varela*, and a Commission witness, was threatened with dismissal by staff officers who accused him

of being 'an interfering faddist.' 'I was standing on the bridge in the evening when the *Medjidieh* arrived in Basra,' he testified. 'She had two steel barges without any protection against the rain, as far as I remember. As this ship, with two barges, came up to us I saw that she was absolutely

packed, and the barges too, with men ... When she was about 300 or 400 yards off it looked as if she was festooned with ropes. The stench when she was close was quite definite, and I found that what I mistook for ropes were dried stalactites of human fæces. The patients were so huddled and

crowded together on the ship that they could not perform the offices of Nature clear of the edge of the ship, and the whole of the ship's side was covered with stalactites of human fæces. This is what I then saw. A certain number of men were standing and kneeling on the immediate perimeter of

the ship. Then we found a mass of men huddled up anyhow—some with blankets and some without. They were lying in a pool of dysentery about 30 feet square. They were covered with dysentery and dejecta generally from head to foot. With regard to the first man I examined, I put

my hand into his trousers, and I thought that he had a hæmorrhage. His trousers were full almost to his waist with something warm and slimy. I took my hand out, and thought it was blood clot. It was dysentery. The man had a fractured thigh, and his thigh was perforated in five or six places.

He had apparently been writhing about the deck of the ship.' In his official telegram, the King regrets that Richard Ayres Ritchie, son of Thomas and Alice Ritchie, husband of Enid Kathleen Ritchie, of 'The Shack', Crowborough, Sussex, age 24, failed to survive the initial assault at

Ctesiphon on November 22nd. With the fury of sixty years of indignation, my grandmother spat out his epitaph: 'His body was flung into the Tigris.' More than half the 235 Indian officers were lost. Of 317 British officers who advanced that day, 130 were killed or wounded. Twenty-three

thousand men were slaughtered or wounded in suicidal offensives to rescue Kut, ten thousand in April alone. India still mourns 'the flower of the Indian army ... buried under the banks of the Tigris from Shu'aiba to Ctesiphon.' The Commission exposed Nixon's cover-up and Hardinge's

complicity: 'There are two methods of concealing a failure. The first is to suppress all mention of it.' The colonials were blamed; spared were the politicians who kept the war going in order to conclude the business at hand, that is, territorial expansion, resource acquisition and aggressive

de-population. John Rutherfurd, a boy of 17, separated from Robert Davers before his mutilation near Fort Detroit in 1763, was also captured by Chippewas. In his account he noted: 'The hunting season being at this time past, the Indians lived upon fish, without either bread, butter, or

salt. This did not agree with my constitution, so that having suffered much from a dysentery, I became so weak as to be unable to walk for seven or eight days, during which time the old man consoled me by telling me that I should not be eaten if I died of that disorder.' Dick's voice had

entered the Royal Albert Hall like sunlight rippling on the sea and now it hovered close to Enid. According to Marjorie, it spoke a reassuring name known only to the two of them. Enid entered the voice. 'Do not worry about me,' it said. 'I feel no pain.' Enid gazed down at herself from the

ceiling. For the first time in months she felt clear and present. A film, like mica, fell away. Nothing *seemed;* she *was* her body. Said the voice, 'I am waiting for you, and for you alone.' Enid was a sky alive with stars. 'I'm proud of you. I'm proud of our son.' The voice faded. She could not bear it.

In it surged—strong, masculine, assured. 'There's one small matter,' it said. Great aunt Marjorie reaches for a cigarette and pushes it into her amber holder. 'His name.' Enid had christened the baby Richard Duncan; everyone called him Dick. The medium began rocking back and forth,

her pupils rolled under their lids. Lips, kissed and unkissed, drew in deep draughts of air. Enid held her breath. On stage the Oxfords moaned. The voice returned, vigorous. 'From here on in, my darling, I beg you, with all my heart, please let him be known as Duncan.' My great aunt sets

fire to her cigarette and inhales deeply. 'For,' and here the voice apparently gathered strength and emotion, 'I want there to be only one Dick in your life.' Marjorie smiles and drains her wine glass. 'Coffee?' From that time forward the boy was known as Duncan. Enid accepted a weekly pension

of five shillings and stayed on in The Shack. Marjorie and her husband sailed home to Vancouver Island and unemployment. Twenty years later their son joined the Air Force; in 1941, while showing a mess-mate how to pass his pilot's exam, the two of them crashed to earth. Eight

hundred and ninety thousand Anglo-Indian boys served in Mespot between 1914–1918, each a tender and beautiful son. What was that song? 'At seventeen, he falls in love quite madly with eyes of tender blue ....' Standing before Cy Twombly's *Quatro Stagioni* on the MOMA mezzanine,

weeping, and I can't say why. These monumental shapes, scrawled upon, savaged by pigment and light, their skins not only registers of, but evidence of time as a tragedy beyond tragedy's knowing, seize and hold me. 'How *dare* one speak of knowing?' they insist, or, 'How dare one

pretend to live?' or, 'How dare one act; one *must*.' In these wrenching, Promethean collisions— picture *Leda*, upstairs, in the grip of sexual fission with the world bull, in swan's down—God is a dreadful comet, bursting from the void in fiery parturition, ravished and bloody, becoming, in turn, ravisher; becoming *us*. In Twombly's unspeakable crime scenes, nothing *seems*, everything *is*. Is rage, desire, coupling, war, beauty, terror, utterance, decay, *is* obliterating joy, is all I tremble to call love. On *Summer*'s surface Twombly retrieves, from the instant's red gut and trembling thorax,

words: '*Ah, it goes, is lost*.' Standing offshore, in a sea of first matter, where vertical is horizontal—in eternity no dimensions—pharaonic barges ply their trade. *Facilis decensus Averno*. The maelstrom leaves its stain. Lord Russell rightly deplored the Mesopotamian invasion as a deliberate

provocation, an act of 'territorial aggrandisement' by 'capitalists, Imperialists and war-mongers.' So he wrote in the pamphlet that landed in him jail in 1916. Imperialism—and not the faulty application of Imperialism—he foresaw, would overreach itself, collapsing into unchecked

opportunism, retaliation and 'a revolution full of violence, hatred and bloodshed, driven by hunger, terror and suspicion—a revolution in which all that is best in Western civilization is bound to perish.' Months later Enid received a package from India. Dick had been brave and

admired. He died instantly, the letter said. In the mouth—Oh! Wilfred Owen. And this: they left the bullet in. Enid's son joined the Navy, later becoming an agent for British Aerospace, now BAE, which armed, then helped destroy, Saddam's Iraq, and which was quick to take its cut of

reconstruction fees. Barthes' father, a Roman Catholic naval officer, perished in a North Sea battle before his son was a year old. The son wrote, 'the past tense of the stroke can also be defined as its future.' He was addressing Twombly. Longing and terror accumulate in our tissue.

We're their precipitate, a form of circuitry—durable, adaptable, combustible—and it seems we witnessed something we should not have. Hence our cytomegalic self-awareness, the teeming, insistent, ravishing, helpless words, marks, or is it larks' wings burned like cries into each child's

'You've got blue eyes;
what else do you want?'

A resident at Cowichan Lodge, near
Duncan, V.I., giving me a hard look.
17 August 2006

Sources

A poem can be a weir, a machine for netting, and ordering—or disordering—voices. In this it operates a little like a transformer, or a voltage booster on a network, and one can only think that it has been operating this way for millennia.

Some of the voices within have been taken from family stories, chance conversations and over-hearings. Others were discovered in the books listed below. Some have no source I can identify; they made themselves known.

I would like to thank the authors and publishers of the following. In cases where I've quoted from letters and other texts, I have tried to be true to the spirit in which they are presented. I am grateful to all the authors below whose research has enriched my understanding.

Oum Kalthoum: A Beneficent Trauma

Adnan, Etel, 'In the Heart of the Heart of Another Country,' *In the Heart of the Heart of Another Country* (San Francisco: City Lights Books, 2005.)

Apes You Sought

Aburish, Saïd K., *Saddam Hussein: The Politics of Revenge* (London: Bloomsbury, 2000).

Benjamin, Walter, 'The Storyteller: Reflections on the Works of Nicolai Leskov,' in *Illuminations: Essays and Reflections*, ed. Hannah Arendt (New York: Schocken Books, 1968).

Borges, Jorge Luis, 'The Paradox of Apollinaire,' in *Selected Non-Fictions*, ed. Eliot Weinberger, trans. Esther Allen, Suzanne Jill Levine and Eliot Weinberger (New York: Viking, 1999).

Breton, André, 'Three Dreams' in *Selections*, ed. and intro. Mark Polizzotti (Berkeley: University of California Press, 2003).

Ellington, Duke, *Music is My Mistress* (New York: Da Capo, 1976).

Hajdu, David, *Lush Life: A Biography of Billy Strayhorn* (New York: Farrar, Straus and Giroux, 1996).

Randall, Lisa, *Warped Passages: Unravelling the Mysteries of the Universe's Hidden Dimensions* (New York: Ecco/HarperCollins Publishers, 2005).

Saunders, Frances Stonor, *Who Paid the Piper? The CIA and the Cultural Cold War* (London: Granta Books, 1999).

van de Leur, Walter, *Something to Live For: The Music of Billy Strayhorn* (New York: Oxford University Press, 2002).

Asking, How

The Gospel of Thomas, intro. Helmut Koester, trans. Thomas O. Lambdin in *The Nag Hammadi Library in English*, ed. James M. Robinson (San Francisco: Harper & Row, Publishers, 1977).

A Valentinian Exposition (XI, 2), with *On the Anointing, on Baptism A and B, and On the Eucharist A and B*, intro. Elaine Pagels, trans. John D. Turner in *The Nag Hammadi Library in English*, ed. James M. Robinson (San Francisco: Harper & Row, Publishers, 1977).

The Pool

Barthes, Roland, 'Interview with *Tel Quel*' in *The Tel Quel Reader*, ed. Patrick ffrench and Roland-François Lack (London: Routledge, 1998).

Chagall, Marc, *My Life*, trans. Elisabeth Abbott (New York: Da Capo Press, 1994).

Gibson, Shimon, *The Cave of John the Baptist* (London: Century, 2004).

Noughts and Crosses

Arnett, Chris, *The Terror of the Coast: Land Alienation and Colonial War on Vancouver Island and the Gulf Islands, 1849–1863* (Vancouver: Talonbooks, 2002).

Burton, Sir Richard, *Love, War and Fancy: The Customs and Manners of the East from Writings on The Arabian Nights*, ed. Kenneth Walker (London: William Kimber & Co, Limited, 1964).

Kapliwatzky, Jochanan, *Arabic Language and Grammar, Part II* (Jerusalem: Rubin Mass, 1942).

'… he had a hunger for eternity.' Charles Lamb, remembering Samuel Taylor Coleridge (d. 25 July, 1834). Written in the album of Mr. Keymer, November 21, 1834. Lamb died on December 27, 1834 at the age of fifty-eight.

McCarthy, Paul, *Céline* (Harmondsworth: Penguin Books, 1977).

Walbran, Captain John T., *British Columbia Coast Names, 1592–1906*, reprinted, intro. G.P.V. Akrigg (North Vancouver: J.J. Douglas Ltd., 1971).

Dislodging: The Colonial Temperament at Cowichan Bay, circa 1900

The Cowichans called Europeans *hwunitums*, or 'the hungry people.' Siwash, the word used by colonists to describe aboriginal people on the west coast circa 1900, is derived from *sauvage*, the term used by Samuel Champlain and his colleagues when, in 1603, they encountered the Montagnais, the Etchemin (Malecite) and the Algonquin people living along the St. Laurent—a term taken up by the French-speaking missionaries who followed him. Champlain's first publication was an account of the 1603 voyage entitled *DES SAUVAGES OU VOYAGE DE SAMUEL CHAMPLAIN DE BROUAGE, FAIT EN LA FRANCE NOUVELLE, L'an mil six cens trois: Contenant: Les moeurs, façon de vivre, mariages, guerres & habitation des Sauvages de Canadas. De la descouverte de plus de quatre cens cinquante lieues dans le païs des Sauvages. Quels peuples y habitent; des animaux qui s'y trouvent; des rivieres, lacs, isles & terres, & quels arbres & fruicts elles produisent. De la coste d'Arcadie, des terres que l'on y a descouvertes, & de plusieurs mines qui y sont, selon le rapport des Sauvages.*

Anderson, Fred, and Andrew Cayton, *The Dominion of War: Empire and Liberty in North America, 1500–2000.* New York: Viking Penguin, 2005.

Cook, Andrew, *The Ace of Spies: The True Story of Sidney Reilly* (Stroud, Gloucestershire: Tempus Publishing Ltd., 2004).

Freud, Sigmund, 'Anxiety and Instinctual Life' in *New Introductory Lectures on Psychoanalysis*, trans. and ed. James Strachey, assisted by Angela Richards (Harmondsworth: Penguin Books/Pelican Freud Library, 1973).

Herman Melville, *Clarel: A Poem and Pilgrimage in the Holy Land* (New York: Hendricks House, 1960).

Overy, Richard, *Interrogations: The Nazi Elite in Allied Hands, 1945* (New York: Penguin Books, 2001).

Service, Robert W., *Ploughman of the Moon: An Adventure into Memory* (New York: Dodd, Mead & Company, 1945).

'men that don't fit in ….' from Robert W. Service, 'The Men That Don't Fit In,' in *Songs of a Sourdough* (Toronto: William Briggs, 1907).

'sore as a boil …' from Robert W. Service, 'The Quitter,' in *Rhymes of a Rolling Stone* (Toronto: William Briggs, 1912).

'My stretcher is one scarlet stain …' from Robert W. Service, 'The Stretcher-Bearer' and 'The Odyssey of 'Erbert 'Iggins,' in *Rhymes of a Red Cross Man* (Toronto: William Briggs, 1916).

'virgin vastitude' from Robert W. Service, 'The Squaw-Man,' in *Songs of the High North* (Toronto: The Ryerson Press, 1970).

Forerunner (I)

'*J'ai baisé ta bouche Iokanaan*' is from the text on Aubrey Beardsley's design for 'The Climax from Oscar Wilde's *Salome.*' Line block print, 1893.

The Post Road

Emily Dickinson's upstairs bedroom faced the Post Road leading into Amherst, Massachusetts. The line, '*It is difficult not to be fictitious in so fair a place …*,' is drawn from a letter Emily Dickinson wrote from Amherst to Thomas Wentworth Higginson in 1868 and first published by him in the *Atlantic Monthly* in 1891. See *Selected Poems and Letters of Emily Dickinson*, ed. and intro. Robert N. Linscott (Garden City: Doubleday Anchor Books, 1959).

Roland Barthes in the Kootenays

What appears here is a revised transcription of a talk presented on 17 May 2003 at 'Alley Alley Home Free': A North American Poetry and Poetics Conference and Festival, in honour of Fred Wah and Pauline Butling, at the University of Calgary in Calgary, Alberta. Many thanks to the organizers and to the editors of *Open Letter* where the earlier version appeared.

Barthes, Roland, 'Interview with *Tel Quel'* in *The Tel Quel Reader*, ed. Patrick ffrench and Roland-François Lack (London: Routledge, 1998).

Half-Measures

This song, with music by composer Neil Weisensel, was written for and sung by Susanna Browne at *Song Room* in Vancouver, B.C., on Feb. 20, 2005. Many thanks to Tom Cone, Karen Matthews and David Pay for creating and hosting *Song Room*.

A Rotary Ricer

To honour his eightieth birthday, this song, with music by Neil Weisensel, was performed for Robin Blaser and invited guests by tenor Frederik Robert and baritone Michael Walker in Vancouver, B.C., on 19 December, 2005.

'... *più angusto vaglio* ...' St John, in the Eighth Heaven, tells Dante, '*Certo a più angusto vaglio / ti conviene schiarar*...,' which is to say, 'To be sure, you must sift with a still finer sieve.' Dante, *Paradiso*, Canto XXVI, 22–23.

'*Orphée, respiro.*' From Glück, '*O del mio dolce ardor.*' The singer whose voice I heard was, in fact, singing the final line of the song, '*Cerco te, chiamo te, spero e sospiro.*' I heard the final words as '*Orphée, respiro,*' mixing French and Italian rather shamelessly.

'... *e vidi Orfeo.*' Dante, *Inferno*, Canto IV, 140.

The Shovel

The Cascadia earthquake, which scientists judge to have had a magnitude of 9.0, occurred in a fault about 80 miles off the Pacific Coast, unleashing a tsunami which is remembered to this day in stories which contemporary listeners often attribute to ancestral memories of Noah's flood. Geologists have calculated that the Cascadia earthquake occurred at 9 p.m. on January 26th, 1700. Much of Lisbon, Portugal, was destroyed by an earthquake on the same day in 1531.

The Anvil

Stage actress Zinaida Raikh was the wife of experimental playwright and theatre director, Vsevolod Meyerhold. On July, 14th, 1939, three weeks after her husband was arrested on trumped-up charges, she was attacked in their apartment. In an act of superstitious cruelty, her eyes were cut out (to prevent her from identifying her assailants), and she was murdered. Reportedly, her body had seventeen knife wounds. The only things missing from the apartment were documents. Meyerhold was tortured incessantly and shot in the back of the head on February 2, 1940.

Amis, Martin. *Koba the Dread: Laughter and the Twenty Million* (New York: Hyperion, 2002).

Chase, William J. *Enemies Within the Gates? The Comintern and the Stalinist Repression, 1934–1939* (New Haven: Yale University Press, 2001).

Darcy, Samuel, 'Dimitrov, Stalin and the 1936 Presidential Elections in the United States.' http://www.revolutionarydemocracy.org/rdv9n1/darcy.htm

Frazer, Chris, 'From Pariahs to Patriots: Canadian Communists and the Second World War.' *Past Imperfect*, Vol. 5, 1996.

Glover, Jonathan, *Humanity: A Moral History of the Twentieth Century* (New Haven and London: Yale University Press, 2000).

Hegel, Georg Wilhelm Friedrich, *Introduction to The Philosophy of History* with an Appendix from *The Philosophy Of Right*, trans. Leo Rauch (Indianapolis: Hackett Publishing Company, Inc., 1988).

History of the Communist Party of the Soviet Union (Bolsheviks), ed. A Commission of the Central Committee of the C.P.S.U. (B.) (Toronto: Francis White Publishers, Ltd., 1939).

Kiernan, V.G., *Poets, Politics and the People*, ed. and intro. Harvey J. Kaye (London: Verso, 1989).

Lenin, V.I., Letter to Gorky, September 15, 1919.

Lipton, Charles, *The Trade Union Movement of Canada 1827–1959* (Montréal: Canadian Social Publications Limited, 1966 (1967).

McEwen, Tom, *The Forge Glows Red: From Blacksmith to Revolutionary* (Toronto: Progress Books, 1974).

Radosh, Ronald, Mary R. Habeck and Grigory Sevostianov, *Spain Betrayed: The Soviet Union in the Spanish Civil War* (New Haven: Yale University Press, 2001).

Siegelbaum, Lewis, and Andrei Sokolov, *Stalinism as a Way of Life* (New Haven: Yale University Press, 2000).

Todorov, Tzvetan, *Hope and Memory*, trans. David Bellos (London: Atlantic Books, 2005).

Fairview

This poem was written to honour George Bowering's seventieth birthday. The geology is taken from Robert Nicholas Spark, 'Crustal thickening and tectonic denudation within the Thor-Odin culmination, Monashee complex, southern Canadian Cordillera.' PhD thesis, University of New Brunswick.

A Square Sonnet

10 February 2006. The tulip tree's in bloom.

North Atlantic Drift

Presented as part of the John Lennon Memorial, Dec. 8, 2005, at the Canadian Memorial United Church and Centre for Peace, Vancouver, B.C.

Over Olean, or The Misuse of Reticence

Aaronsohn, Alexander, *With the Turks in Palestine* (Boston: Houghton Mifflin, 1916).

Aboul-Enein, Youssef, 'The First World War Mesopotamian Campaigns: Military Lessons on Iraqi Ground Warfare,' *Strategic Insights*, Vol. IV, Issue 6, June 2005.

Aburish, Saïd K., *Saddam Hussein: The Politics of Revenge* (London: Bloomsbury, 2000).

Aldington, Richard, *Lawrence of Arabia: A Biographical Enquiry* (Chicago: Henry Regnery Company, 1955).

Ali, Tariq, *Bush in Babylon: The Recolonisation of Iraq* (London: Verso, 2003).

Antonius, George, *The Arab Awakening* (Beirut: Librairie du Liban, 1969).

Barker, A.J., *The Bastard War: The Mesopotamian Campaign of 1914–1918* (New York: The Dial Press, 1967).

Barthes, Roland, *The Responsibility of Forms: Critical Essays on Music, Art, and Representation*, trans. Richard Howard (New York: Farrar Straus & Giroux, 1984).

Bell, Alexander Graham, *Obituary*, 'Dr. Bell, Inventor of Telephone, Dies / Sudden End, Due to Anemia, Comes in Seventy-Sixth Year at His Nova Scotia Home / Notables Pay Him Tribute / Lived to See Speech Reproduced Across the World—Pioneered in Aeronautics,' *The New York Times*, August 3, 1922.

Bey, Comandant M. Moukbil, *La Campagne de l'Irak, 1914–1918* (Paris: Editions Berger-Levrault,1933).

Boas, Franz, 'Modern Populations of America' (1915), in Franz Boas, *Race, Language and Culture* (New York: The Free Press, 1966).

Boulez, Pierre, 'Poetry—Centre and Absence—Music' and 'Sound, Word, Synthesis', *Orientations* (Cambridge: Harvard University Press, 1986).

Braddon, Russell, *The Siege* (London: Jonathan Cape, 1969).

Breton, André, *Conversations: The Autobiography of Surrealism*, trans, and intro. Mark Polizzotti, (New York: Marlowe & Company, 1993).

Carver, Field Marshall Lord, *The National Army Museum Book of the Turkish Front 1914–1918* (London: Pan Books in association with The National Army Museum, 2004).

Chaplin, Charles, *My Autobiography* (New York: Simon and Schuster, 1964).

Cutlack, Frederick Morley, *The Australian Flying Corps in the Western and Eastern Theatres of War 1914–1918*, Vol. VIII of *The Official History of Australia in the War of 1914–1918*, 4th ed. (Sydney: Angus and Robertson: 1935).

Dahl, Erik. J, 'Naval Innovation: From Coal to Oil,' *Joint Force Quarterly*, Winter 2000–2001.

Eliot, Valerie (ed.), *The Letters of T.S. Eliot, Volume I: 1898–1922* (New York: Harcourt Brace Jovanovich, Publishers, 1988).

Ferguson, Niall, *The Pity of War* (New York: Basic Books, 1999).

Fisk, Robert, 'Iraq, 1917', http://www.informationclearinghouse.info/article6337.htm.

Fisk, Robert, *The Great War for Civilisation: The Conquest of the Middle East* (London: Harper Perennial, 2006).

Foreman, Lewis (Ed.), *Oh My Horses! Elgar and the Great War. The Music of Elgar, Vol.2* (Lower Broadheath: Elgar Editions, n.d.). Letter from Elgar to Frank Schuster, August 25, 1914.

Forster, E.M. 'Some people would say ....': Letter from E.M. Forster to Sir Henry John Newbolt, 7 Nov. 1915. David J. Holmes Autographs.

Fromkin, David. *A Peace to End All Peace: The Fall of the Ottoman Empire and the Creation of the Modern Middle East.* (New York: Henry Holt and Company, 1989).

Gardner, Nikolas, 'Sepoys and the Siege of Kut-al-Amara, December 1915–April 1916,' *War in History*, Volume 11, Issue 3, 2004.

Gay, Peter, *Freud: A Life for Our Time* (New York: W.W. Norton & Company, 1977).

Goold, Douglas. 'Lord Hardinge and the Mesopotamia Expedition and Inquiry, 1914–1917,' *The Historical Journal*, Vol. 19, No. 4, 1976, pp. 919–945.

Hemingway, Ernest, *A Moveable Feast* (New York: Charles Scribner's Sons, 1964).

Herbert, Aubrey. *Mons, Anzac & Kut* (London: Hutchison & Co. Ltd, 1919).

Hoare, Philip, *Oscar Wilde's Last Stand: Decadence, Conspiracy, and the Most Outrageous Trial of the Century* (New York: Arcade Publishing, 1998).

Ibn 'Arabi, Muhyi-d-din, *The Wisdom of the Prophets (Fusus al-Hikam)*, trans. Titus Burckhardt [Arabic to French] and Angela Culme-Seymour [French to English] (Gloucestershire: Beshara Publications, 1975).

Lawrence, D.H., *The Collected Letters of D.H. Lawrence*, Vol. 1, ed. and intro Harry T. Moore (London: Heinemann, 1965).

Lawrence, T.E., *The Letters of T.E. Lawrence*, ed. David Garnett (New York: Doubleday, Doran & Company, 1939).

Lenin, V.I., *Revolution at the Gates: A Selection of Writings of Lenin from February to October 1917*, ed. with introduction and afterword by Slavoj Zizek (London: Verso, 2002).

'The Mesopotamian Half Flight Diary,' australianflyingcorps.org, http://www.australianflying-corps.org/2002_1999/afc_squadron_mesopotamian_diary.htm.

Miller, Lt. Col. E.D., *Lecture on Horse Management on Active Service* (Lowestoft: Flood, 1918).

Milton, Joyce, *Tramp: The Life of Charlie Chaplin* (New York: HarperCollinsPublishers, 1996).

Nusseibeh, Sari, *Once Upon a Country: A Palestinian Life*, with Anthony David (New York: Farrar, Strauss and Giroux, 2007).

Pope, Stephen, and Elizabeth-Anne Wheal, *The Macmillan Dictionary of The First World War* (London: Macmillan, 1997).

Reguer, Sara, 'Cheap Oil and the First Lord: A Chapter in the Career of Winston Churchill,' *Military Affairs*, Vol. 46, No. 3., October 1982.

Report of the Mesopotamia Commission, Part X.—Medical Breakdown, D. The Misuse of Reticence (London: H.M. Stationary Office, 1917).

Riley, Cam, 'The Mesopotamian Half-Flight', Feb. 28, 2006, http://www.australianflying corps.org/story/2006/2/28/10595/1308.

Russell, Bertrand, *The Autobiography of Bertrand Russell, 1914–1944* (Boston: Little, Brown and Company, 1968).

Sachar, Howard M., *The Emergence of the Middle East, 1914–1924* (London: Allen Lane, The Penguin Press, 1969).

Seymour-Jones, Carole, *Painted Shadow: A Life of Vivienne Eliot* (New York: Nan A. Talese/ Doubleday, 2004).

Singha, Radhika, 'Iraq: on duty once again?' *The Hindu* Magazine (Chennai), Sunday, Mar 21, 2004.

Stevenson, David, *Cataclysm: The First World War as Political Tragedy* (New York: Basic Books, 2004).

Tate, James W., Frank Clifford Harris and Valentine, 'A Bachelor Gay', from *The Maid of the Mountains*, lyrics by Harry Graham, music by Harold Fraser-Simson, book by Frederick Lonsdale, with additional lyrics by Frank Clifford Harris and Valentine. Additional numbers by James W. Tate (London: Ascherberg, Hopwood & Crew, Ltd., 1917). First performed at Daly's Theatre, London, on Saturday, February 10th, 1917.

Tomalin, Claire, *Thomas Hardy: The Time-Torn Man* (London: Viking, 2006).

von Unworth, Matthew, *Freud's Requiem: Mourning, Memory, and the Invisible History of a Summer Walk* (New York: Riverhead Books, 2005).

Whiting, John D., 'Jerusalem's Locust Plague: Being a Description of the Recent Locust Influx into Palestine, and Comparing Same with Ancient Locust Invasions as Narrated in the Old World's History Book, the Bible.' *The National Geographic Magazine*, Vol. XXVIII, No. 6, December 1915.

Yapp, Nick, *gettyimages 1910s: Decades of the 20th Century* (Köln: Könemann Verlagsgesellschaft GmbH, 2001).